TRACK DOWN
YOUR
ANCESTORS

TRACK DOWN
YOUR
ANCESTORS

AND DRAW UP
YOUR FAMILY TREE

Estelle Catlett

RIGHT WAY

Typeset in 10/12pt Times by County Typesetters, Margate, Kent.
Printed and bound in Great Britain by Cox & Wyman Ltd., Reading, Berkshire.

The *Right Way* series and the *Paperfronts* series are both published by Elliot Right Way Books, Brighton Road, Lower Kingswood, Tadworth, Surrey, KT20 6TD, U.K.

CONTENTS

LIST OF ILLUSTRATIONS

1
LOOKING FOR YOUR ANCESTORS

This book assumes that you have no knowledge at all of family history research, that you are a complete but enthusiastic beginner. It will take you step by step through the process of tracing your own family history. I would ask you to read the book through first so that you will have some idea of what you are about to undertake, then to return to the beginning and follow the suggested assignments through, chapter by chapter.

Who are you? You are the present day accumulation of all the genes, characteristics and hereditary behaviour of your ancestors. Have you ever wondered who your ancestors were, where they lived and what they did? What they looked like?

Heredity is not exclusive to anyone. We all have ancestors and we all have sagas to tell. Everybody can enjoy this hobby. The dustman and the duke, the ordinary person as much as royalty is able equally to research his or her own family history. It is not an area exclusively owned by the nobility although, of course, in the writings of history, opinions as to whose families matter the most will always differ.

Over the past 40 years the growth of this leisure activity, which seems to reflect a romantic nostalgia for the past, has astounded professional researchers. This development has been both beneficial and stimulating. Men and women work at their researches, introducing into what used to be a recreation a certain amount of professionalism. Information has spread worldwide and the chances of finding out more about remote branches of your family are increased because your distant relative, hitherto unknown to you, has also been working away researching his family history and you can exchange your knowledge to each other's benefit. Even more exciting is that it has become worldwide, perhaps because of the increasing ease of communications made available to us by our electronic age.

In order to research your own family history you will have to be a detective, looking for clues and sifting the evidence available. Perseverance, luck, careful correct copying and note taking are all essential. There can never be a guarantee of success, but you will always find it a challenging and satisfying hobby. It takes time and is a slow process but it is well worth all the effort put into it. With persistence and a degree of luck you will be able to trace your family roots back to the late 1700's and possibly even further. I experienced an extreme example of luck recently when I required the assistance of an American researcher. Using my list of professional researchers, covering the whole of America and the 'pin' method I wrote to an unknown genealogist in the State where I required a search. The work was quickly and efficiently completed and when the documents were sent to me the letter accompanying them also told me that my professional colleague had an ancestor with the same surname as myself (my husband's family surname) whose family originated in Kent in England. The name is unusual and I was able to confirm that my husband's family did indeed originate in Kent. I am now awaiting a copy of my American colleague's own family tree to see if we can make a connection somewhere. The patron saint of genealogists must have guided my 'pin' that day.

If you can one day show your family a well presented

and interesting history they will be delighted. Do not doubt it. You will also gain great satisfaction and pleasure from a job well done and have something to pass on to your children who may well be bitten by the bug and continue the research. It is endless. As members of your family are born, marry or die, so the information to add to your research grows.

Before you start, go to the library and borrow biographies of famous people. You will find them interesting to read and they will give you some ideas on how to start and what you are looking for. Your own family history is as interesting as anyone else's, whether famous or not. There are also Family History Societies in existence. Go to a meeting of your local society – your library will probably know where and when they meet. They will welcome you as a newcomer and give advice and you will meet people who have the same interest as yourself.

How and where do you start? First talk to your family and tell them what you are doing. Write to your cousin in Australia or your aunt in Scotland. It may be that someone else in your family is engaged in family history research and has done some of the work for you. They will produce all sorts of bits and pieces which may prove useful (if not immediately then perhaps later when they slot into a space and confirm some piece of research which you have been following).

Gather up all the information you can from your family before you start. It may provide clues and help which will save you a great deal of time. Old letters, postcards and birthday cards in particular are very helpful. Articles from newspapers, letters from abroad, wills and diaries can provide dates and names that you are looking for.

Before it is too late, talk to your older relatives and make a note of what they tell you. There is nothing that old people like to do better than talk about "the old days".

They will, while reminiscing about past events and places, reveal much information to help you. They may need gentle prompting as to exact names, dates and occasions. Don't be afraid to ask them, encourage them and they will be a mine of information. Personal knowledge will often reveal unknown relationships but they must always be checked and supported by documentation if your family history is to be based on fact.

If you find it difficult to write quickly and keep up with what is being said, invest in a small personal tape recorder, the type which is not intrusive, which you can hold in your hand or lay on a table. They are not too expensive and you can save all the information to go through at a later date when you have more time. Some people may object to the use of a tape recorder and "dry up" but most will soon forget its presence and talk freely. Your only difficulty will be to change the tape quickly enough so as not to miss anything that is being said.

A word of warning, do not take everything that members of your family tell you as fact. They may choose not to tell you about one particular person whom they disliked or with whom they quarrelled or who they consider is a disgrace to the family. There may have been incidents in the past which they do not wish to remember. Memories are often hazy as to dates and places. They are also coloured by happy or sad experiences. Memory plays funny tricks. We all have some things we would rather forget. It may be those very things that you will need to know. Everything should be checked where possible by following up information given. If several members of the family tell the same story it probably is true, but not always. It may have been handed down by tradition and the facts changed by each story teller to suit the occasion. It is for you to discover the answers.

Some families have family bibles in which generations

of names and dates have been recorded. Possibly one of your older aunts or a grandparent has it pushed away in a cupboard. Although it is not on display, they will not want to part with it. You may have to copy the entries. If you do, make sure you copy them exactly, even if you think the spelling is incorrect. If you have difficulty reading the handwriting ask other members of the family if they remember any of the names. If you can persuade the owner to part with the bible for a short time, take it to a shop to have the relevant pages photocopied. Most towns have "copy shops" charging a small sum per page for copies. If you return the bible promptly the owner will know you are to be trusted and may produce other treasured documents for you to see.

Old photographs and photograph albums can be a source of much information. Very often notes of the people in the photographs or places and dates where they were taken will be found written on the back. If there was an enthusiastic photographer in the family who kept their work in an album, they probably wrote all the details beside each picture. This could prove a great source of information.

When you have gathered all the available details you should have many pages of your notebook filled, or several small tapes waiting to be played at your leisure and you will probably have renewed acquaintance with a few distant relatives who were no doubt very pleased to hear from you. Family history research can result in many happy reunions with those we thought were lost to us and introductions to those we did not know existed.

It is no use jumping into the middle just because you have some odd pieces of information about distant relatives. You can only start with the information about which you are certain, so begin with yourself and work back into the past. If you have an uncommon name or a family name that is passed down from one generation to another, then it will be much easier, but you may find that your name, which you thought was unusual is in fact very common in some other part of the country. This may be a helpful point of reference but could lead you on a time-consuming and wasteful exercise unless you are sure there is some connection.

Remember to keep ALL the notes that you make, even those on scraps of paper and the backs of envelopes. You never know when they may come in useful. It is also essential to make a note of where you obtained the specific pieces of information in case you ever need to check the notes you made or refer again to a particular book or documents. Cite the exact source of the information and give all the data you have at the time you make your notes. If you copy information from the family bible, it is not sufficient to mark your notes "from the family bible". You may not remember who has possession of the bible or where it is housed. Make a full note of the date on which the notes were taken, in whose possession the bible remains and the address. It is particularly important to make a note of your sources of reference when visiting registries, libraries, museums or newspaper archives. You may have spent a great deal of time tracking down the information. If you know where you found it, the next time you need to refer to it a great deal of wasted time and frustration will be avoided if you know where to look. The following are examples of good and bad reference notes. For the purpose of these examples you are the family historian "John Smith".

BAD	GOOD
"Letter from Aunt Annie"	Letter from Mrs. Annie Goodall dated 27 January 1985 to John Smith (family historian). Letter now in possession of John Smith filed under reference G/29.

BAD	GOOD
"Family Bible"	Copied by John Smith, 19 January 1984 from family Bible record of Arthur Smith of Harrogate b. 2 November 1867. Bible in possession of Harold G. Smith of 22 Grace Street, Harrogate. Original entries in Bible hand written, authors unknown. Photocopies in possession of John Smith filed under reference S/6.
BAD	GOOD
"Book in Guildhall Library"	Information copied 2 March 1983 by John Smith from book "Gleaning History" by S. R. Green. Published by Fish & Sons. Book available at Guildhall Library, London. Library reference No. 86/B7.
BAD	GOOD
"A death certificate"	Information copied by John Smith 6 May 1985 from death certificate of Constance Ellen Harris d. 29 October 1899. Original in possession of Alice Cross (daughter of C. E. Harris) of 22 Cramery Road, Northampton. Photocopy in possession of John Smith filed under reference H/219.

All families do not have "skeletons in the cupboard" nor a banished "black sheep" but it is much more interesting if they do. Not many people can boast a highwayman or an illegitimate Earl as a distant ancestor, but you may be surprised by the occupations and connections of your forebears. I have met many who through their research claim a family association with the royal family, Princess Diana, the Churchill family or one of the great families of Europe, however tenuous the link may be. Most families, however, even if they have a tradition of being town dwellers will find roots somewhere in the countryside.

A little like a jigsaw puzzle, start at the outside edges and work inwards as you find the pieces that fit together. It may take a long time to find the one piece that will enable you to proceed further but do not give up. You may lose your way and feel discouraged. You may decide to give up the research for a time, possibly a few months, or even years. It doesn't matter, it is always there for you to return to. The chances are, however, that once you start you will find it difficult to stop. It will be your own personal serial or "soap opera"; you will feel compelled to know "what happened next".

One more thing to decide before you go any further is which branch of your family you are first going to follow. The further you go the more branches your family tree will have and those branches will divide into smaller branches and eventually into twigs, each bearing a name and a relationship to the others. If you start with yourself, your family name will usually be the same as that of your father. Before they married your mother's family name was different from that of your father, so that immediately you have two family names to follow. By the time you get to your grandparents you will have four family names to research and when you reach your great grandparents you will have eight different family names. The diagram (Fig. 1) gives an illustration.

Most people follow their father's family name when they start, following through with the male line only. This is called the paternal line. If you follow your mother's family, that is your maternal line. It is easier to start on your

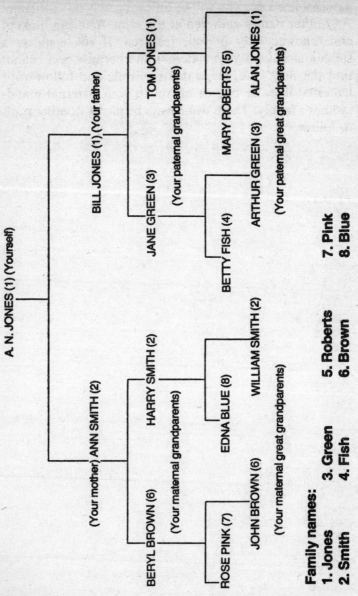

Fig 1. Family Tree as far back as your great-Grandparents.

paternal line since you will be following only one surname. Any other names gathered at the same time can be kept and followed later in your research. If you come to a sudden stop with your paternal line because you cannot find the next clue, leave it for a while and follow your maternal line, or branch off on to your paternal grandmother's family. There will always be plenty of other trails to follow.

2
THE GENERAL REGISTRY

When you have gathered all the existing information from your family, store it safely and start at the beginning with yourself. Do you have a copy of your own birth certificate? Get it out and look at it. What does it tell you? It gives you the following information:

1. Your date and place of birth.
2. Your name.
3. Your sex.
4. Your father's name and surname.
5. Your mother's name and maiden name (her surname before she was married).
6. Your father's occupation.
7. The name and description of the person giving the information of your birth and their address.
8. The date of registration.
9. The district in which you were registered.
10. The sub-district in which you were registered.
11. The County in which you were registered.

If you were born in England or Wales after 1968 your birth certificate will also show the birthplace of both your parents and the previous name of your mother if different from her maiden name. If, for instance she had been widowed or divorced and remarried then her previous married surname would also be given.

Your birth certificate as a starting point gives you a great

17

deal of information. Armed with that information you are
on your way to a thrilling journey into the past.

If you do not have a copy of your birth certificate you
can obtain one from the Registrar of Births, Deaths and
Marriages. There are separate registries for England and
Wales, Scotland, Northern Ireland and the Irish Republic.
All the addresses are given in the Appendix to this book.

Write to the Chief Registrar giving as much detail as
you can. Your full name, exact date and place of birth. If
you know your father's full name and your mother's
maiden name give that information. In England and Wales
if you are able to go to the registry to make the application
yourself a copy certificate will cost less than if you request
the Registry staff to make a search on your behalf and
you can collect the copy within two or three days. If you
have to write, the cost is considerably more for each certificate and it can take as long as three weeks before you
receive that elusive document. Charges and length of waiting time vary from registry to registry.

Registration of births, deaths and marriages in England
and Wales became compulsory on the 1st July 1837. In
Scotland registration commenced on 1st January 1855 and
in Ireland in 1864. All entries in the Register are indexed
alphabetically and by searching the indexes you should be
able to find the details and obtain the certificates you
require. It should therefore in theory be easy to trace your
family history at least back to the dates of compulsory
registration with little difficulty. It should be, but it is not
always so. That is what makes it so interesting. If it were
a matter of simply going to the registries with a list of
names and dates it would soon become repetitious and
boring, but somewhere along the line you will "lose" someone and you will have to start looking elsewhere. That is
when you become a detective and when the information
you have gathered from your family can be used as a
reference.

If you live in or near London and your first searches relate to people who lived or are living in England and Wales, it is well worth a visit to the Office of Population Census and Surveys at St. Catherine's House, part of which houses the index search rooms for Births, Deaths and Marriages. You will, over the course of your research, return many times. Your first visit is always exciting but can be bewildering if you do not know what to do or where to look. Provide yourself with a good notebook – the type used for shorthand or an exercise book – and plenty of pencils with a pencil sharpener with its own box for the pencil shavings. Many registries, libraries and archives do not allow the use of ball point pens and insist on the use of pencils only. If you make a practice of using pencils everywhere, you can't go wrong. A useful 'travel pack' to take with you when carrying out any form of research should contain pencils, pencil sharpener and eraser, a magnifying glass (particularly useful when researching early original documents) and plenty of small change for use in copying machines where they are available. On your first visit to St. Catherine's House allow yourself a whole day so that you have plenty of time. Wear casual clothes and comfortable shoes, you will be standing most of the day.

As you enter St. Catherine's House through the revolving doors, on the right is the enquiry desk and to the left are the security personnel. In front of you are the search rooms. There is no entry fee and no search fees to pay if you carry out your own researches. There are attendants who will direct you if you cannot find what you are looking for, but they are not usually available to assist individuals with their own personal searches.

The first thing you will realise is that you are not alone in your interest in family history research. The Registry is always full of people looking for their ancestry. You will hear Australian, American, West Indian, Canadian,

Indian, Scots and Irish accents as well as English. The Registry is always crowded with both professional and amateur searchers of all ages. Not all family historians are maiden aunts, retired colonels and housewives, many are young. The one thing they all have in common is enthusiasm. In the summer holiday months the number of searchers is increased by visitors from abroad and students on holiday. Most, but not all, researchers are friendly. They are all absorbed in their own research, but sometimes do not object to being asked for advice – they may even offer it! A delighted cry of "found it" can often be heard when a dedicated but tired searcher's patience is rewarded. Sympathetic smiles and nods of encouragement will greet that lucky person. Do not be intimidated by obviously experienced searchers – they were all beginners themselves once.

Before you start your searches, walk through the registry so that you know where things are. The registry is divided into three large rooms. Each room has banks of shelves containing many volumes which index alphabetically all the entries contained in the registers. The first search room contains red indexes for births on the right and black death indexes on the left. A side room off the death indexes also houses some birth records. Walk forward to the end of the room, up a few steps and to your left are more death records. In front of you is the desk where you can collect certificates which were previously ordered and the Supervisor's Office where they will deal with any specific enquiries. To the right are the cashiers' booths where certificates are ordered and paid for and the desk where application forms for certificates can be obtained. At the end of the cashiers' booths are swing doors. Immediately through those doors to the left are the toilets. Walk down the corridor and turn left by the telephones for the green marriage indexes. Directions are clearly marked. Also in that area are the Miscellaneous records.

You will not be allowed to see the original registers. You must search the indexes to find the details of the entry that you require and then apply for the certificate. The volumes in each search area are housed in banks of shelves each three shelves high. The upright at the end of each bank of shelves is clearly marked showing the dates of the volumes contained and between the banks of shelves are long desks at which you can stand, where the volumes can be rested while you search. There are no seats, so be prepared to stand in fairly crowded conditions. There is a small section with seats and low desks provided for disabled people. The volumes are large and heavy and some have canvas handles on the spine to assist when taking them from the shelves. The earlier volumes are hand written, the later ones are typewritten or printed.

In each section, births, marriages and deaths, each year is divided into quarters. March, June, September and December. The quarters are divided as follows:

March quarter entries   January, February, March
June quarter entries   April, May, June
September quarter entries   July, August, September
December quarter entries   October, November,
                               December

Each quarter is divided alphabetically so that for some years, when there were more births, marriages or deaths there are more volumes. For some years there may be only four volumes: March A–Z, June A–Z, September A–Z and December A–Z. In others each quarter may be divided into several volumes such as:

March A–F, March G–L, March M–R, March S–Z,
June A–D, June E–K, June L–R, June S–Z
September A–E, September F–P, September R–Z
December A–K, December L–R, December S–Z
giving a total of fourteen volumes for that year.

Birth Certificates

As an example, let us look for your birth certificate in the red volumes. You know your name, date of birth and roughly where your birth occurred. First find the bank of shelves showing the date you require and walk along until you come to the exact year. Remember there are three rows of shelves, only the middle shelf is at eye level. Look for the quarter in which your birth took place and then the volume containing the letter of the alphabet with which your surname begins in that quarter. If your name is Joan Shepheard and you were born in August 1920 you would look for the volume marked 1920 September S. If you are Henry Arthur Brown born in April 1908 you would look for the volume marked 1908 June B.

Take the volume from the shelf (you may have to wait if someone else has that volume out) and put it on a space nearest to you on the desk. You will have to fit in with the other searchers, spaces are jealously guarded. Look through the book until you come to the page showing the surname you require. The pages are alphabetically indexed at the top left hand and right hand corners so that you can quickly find the page you need. The indexes will show the name of the persons, the district where registered, the volume and page in the register as follows:

Surname	District	Volume	Page
Shepheard Joan	Barnsley	9a	666
or			
Brown Henry Arthur	Hackney	21	271

The district of registration is the local area registry or county registry and is not always the exact place of birth. It is as well to know the names of the surrounding towns or boroughs in case you have a fairly common surname.

Remember also that registration of an event may not necessarily take place on the same date as the event. In the case of a birth the time allowed for registration is forty-two days. Registration could therefore have taken place some time later, so that if you are looking for an event which occurred in September it may be recorded in either the September or the December quarter. The only thing of which you can be certain is that it could not have been recorded in the June quarter before the event took place.

Once you are sure you have the right person, and if you start with yourself it should not be too difficult, copy all the information into your notebook taking care to get the numbers and letters of the volume and pages correct.

Try another exercise with your father's birth. You will need to know his full name, date and place of birth. Information as to the maiden name of the mother is only required for births registered after the September quarter of the year 1911. The important details are the volume and page so make sure you get the numbers correct. One digit wrong and you will not get your certificate, or you may get the wrong one – an expensive and time-consuming mistake. You are now ready to make the application for a copy of the entry in the register. Go to the desk in front of the cashiers' booths where you will find supplies of application forms. The application forms for a full birth certificate are coloured pink and are numbered CAS 51. Instructions for how to complete the forms are clearly printed on them. Complete box A as in Figure 2 overleaf and box B exactly the same as box A. Sign the form and print your name and address in block capitals. If you have any difficulty, an attendant may be able to assist you.

Take your completed form to a cashier together with the fee. If you are able to collect the certificate yourself the cashier will give you a receipt and will tell you when you can return to collect the certificate which is usually within three days. Do not lose the receipt. Receipts are issued in different colours and are used to identify your

When you have found the entry, **copy the names and particulars from the index into the spaces A and B below in BLOCK CAPITALS**

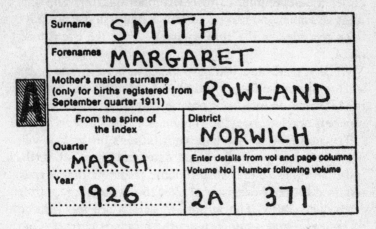

Surname	SMITH
Forenames	MARGARET
Mother's maiden surname (only for births registered from September quarter 1911)	ROWLAND

From the spine of the index	District
	NORWICH
Quarter MARCH	Enter details from vol and page columns
	Volume No. / Number following volume
Year 1926	2A / 371

Now complete the rest of the form and take it to one of the

Fig. 2 Application Form for a Birth Certificate – Example of Box A
Completed for Birth of Margaret Smith, January 1926

certificate when you collect it from the front desk. If you wish the certificate to be posted you will be given an envelope to address to yourself and will probably be told that the delay will be about two to three weeks. In practice certificates sent by mail usually take about ten days.

Death Certificates
   A death certificate will give the following information:
1. Date and place of death.
2. Name and surname.
3. Sex.
4. Age at death.
5. Occupation.

6. Cause of death.
7. Name of Informer.
8. Qualification of Informer
   (relationship to deceased).
9. Date of registration.

Certificates issued for deaths after 1969 will also give the date and place of birth of the deceased, the maiden name of a woman if married and the usual address of the informant. In particular the date and place of birth can be very helpful.

The indexes of the death registers can be searched in the same way as those for births. From 1865 the age at death is given in the index so that if there are two people with the same name the age of death can help to pinpoint the one you are looking for. If you know roughly how old the person was when they died and the age of death shown is many years different it is probably the wrong person.

The application forms for death certificates are numbered CAS 52 and are coloured lavender. They should be completed in the same way as the applications for birth certificates by completing boxes A and B and the other requested information. (Figure 3, page 26.)

Marriage Certificates
A marriage certificate will give you the following information:
1. Date
2. Names and surnames of the bride and groom
3. Ages of the bride and groom
4. Descriptions (spinster, bachelor etc.)
5. Professions
6. Addresses
7. Name of the fathers of both parties
8. Occupation of both fathers
9. Names of witnesses

When you have found the entry, **copy the names and particulars from the index into the spaces A and B below in BLOCK CAPITALS**

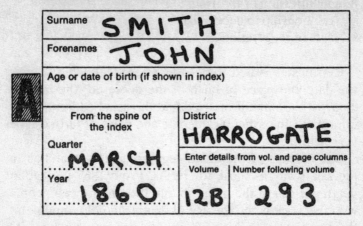

Surname	SMITH
Forenames	JOHN

Age or date of birth (if shown in index)

From the spine of the index	District
	HARROGATE
Quarter	
MARCH	Enter details from vol. and page columns
	Volume	Number following volume
Year	
1860	12B	293

Now complete the rest of the form and take it to one of the

Fig. 3 Application Form for a Death Certificate – Example of Box A
Completed for John Smith who died January 1860

The green indexes are searched in a similar manner. One advantage is that you can cross check that you have the correct marriage by looking in the same quarter under the names of both the bride and groom. If the volume and page numbers are the same for each, you have the correct marriage entry and can proceed to apply for a copy certificate on the green printed application forms. If the marriage took place from 1984 onwards, no quarter is shown on the index volumes. There is a column beside the names, headed 'REG' and that reference should be entered on your application form instead of the quarter in the special box provided. ('REG' is an internal reference used by the Registry.)

If you are married, look for your own entry, if not look

for that of your parents. All you need to know are the names of the groom, the maiden name of the bride, the date and place of the marriage. The place is not quite so essential since if you have both names you can cross check that you have the correct entry and the index will give you the district of the registry. Make an application for the marriage certificate of yourself or your parents on the green coloured form numbered CAS 53, completing box A and box B as shown in Figure 4. The details given on that certificate will provide you with information which will enable you to continue your searches.

Additional records contained at St. Catherine's House are for births and deaths at sea, records kept by British

When you have found the entry, **copy the names and particulars from the index into the spaces A and B below in BLOCK CAPITALS**

	Surname	Forenames
Man	**BROWN**	**ROBERT**
Woman	**SMITH**	**JOAN**

From the spine of the index	District **PUTNEY**
YEAR **1936**	
QUARTER **MARCH**	Enter details from vol and page columns
	Volume No. | Number following volume
FROM 1984 BOUND ANNUAL INDEXES DO NOT SHOW A QUARTER ENTER DETAILS FROM COLUMN HEADED REG	**9A** | **123**
REG	

Now complete the rest of the form and take it to one of the

Fig. 4 Application Form for a Marriage Certificate – Example of Box A
Completed for Marriage of Robert Brown and Joan Smith, February 1936

Consuls abroad since 1849, some Army records for personnel as well as their families since 1761 and Royal Air Force returns commencing in 1920.

A two-tier charging system for postal applications operates at St. Catherine's House, whereby a researcher will be charged a lower fee when quoting the exact index volume reference for the certificate required. If a search is involved, a higher fee will be charged. The object of this two-tier system is to encourage the use of microfilm copies of the St. Catherine's House indexes which are now widely available for use in local record offices and libraries. The OPCS publish a free small but useful booklet giving instructions about how to use the facilities at St. Catherine's House.

This chapter has assumed that you have experienced no difficulty in finding the entries you require. In the next chapter we will discuss how to proceed if you cannot find the entries for which you are looking. We will also find out where the information can lead and where to search if your family comes from Scotland or Ireland.

3
OTHER REGISTRIES

In addition to the indexes for births, marriages and deaths, St. Catherine's House holds other indexes housed under the subject name of Miscellaneous.

These cover British subjects who were born, married or died abroad including deaths in the air and at sea. However, they only cover those events when they were registered at the nearest British Consulate. In addition there are some Army registers. These events are not fully indexed and are not a complete record, but should be considered when looking for a 'missing' relative. The volumes in this section are on shelves in the same area as the death registers. Each is labelled showing the contents, such as "H.M. Ships Marriages 1849–1889" and "Deaths in the air 1945–1970". There are about 18 of these volumes all containing different information. The indexes are colour coded similarly to the general indexes, red for births, green for marriages and black for deaths.

Also on the Miscellaneous shelves are indexes for Foreign Registers kept by British Clergymen abroad, some of which are very old, the oldest being "Belgium, Baptisms and burials 1817–1850." The countries covered by these registers which include births, marriages and deaths are Belgium, Burma, China, Denmark, India, Japan, Mesopotamia (Iraq), Palestine (Israel), Portugal, Roumania, Russia, Sweden and parts of France, Germany, Holland and Italy. They cover various years, some spanning from 1840–1947 and relate to some of the British living in those countries, but by no means all of them. Copies of all these certificates should be applied for on the blue forms provided at the desk near the indexes. The forms are printed in red (births), green (marriages) and black (deaths) and are completed in a similar manner to those for the general entries. Some of the overseas indexes are not on the shelves. If you cannot find the one you require, ask at the front desk. You will be given a pass and taken to the overseas section by an attendant where you can see all the overseas indexes.

Records of still-births in England and Wales commenced on 1 July 1927. Application for special permission has to be made to the Registrar General if a copy of the record is required.

Copies of entries from the other Miscellaneous registers are applied for on special forms and by special procedures. Help in completing these forms should be sought from one of the official assistants on duty.

Adoptions

There were no official adoption certificates before 1920 and the records at St. Catherine's House commence on 1st January 1927. Indexes for adoption certificates show only the adoptive name and the names of the adopting parents. They do not give the name of the person before adoption. They do give the correct date of birth and are therefore similar to a normal birth certificate, except that the surname shown is not the name at birth. Some children were adopted by close relatives in which case the surname could possibly be the same, but the certificate would not reveal this.

Only an adult adopted person can obtain a copy of the original birth certificate showing the name of the natural parents. A substantial amount of information is required in order to obtain such a certificate. The date of the adoption, the court where the order was made, the full names and surname of the adoptive parents and the name of the child (adoptive surname). For adoptions up to and including 12th November 1975 an adopted person requiring their original birth certificate would have to see and be counselled by a social worker before the information was made available to them. For adoptions after 12th November 1975 the person has a choice whether to be counselled or not. Written application must be made.

Scotland

Family historians whose families have roots in Scotland have an advantage over those whose records are in England and Wales.

Scottish civil registration did not commence until 1st January 1855 but their record keeping was much more thorough than that of England and Wales. All the certificates of births, marriages and deaths contain more information than the English certificates.

Birth certificates give, in addition to the information on the English certificates, one important addition, the date and place of the parents' marriage. This enables the searcher to obtain a copy marriage certificate for the parents without having to search the indexes quarter by quarter, year by year from the date of the child's birth to find the marriage date. Marriage certificates give the names of both parents of the bride and the groom, not only that of the father as their English counterparts. Death certificates give the names of both parents of the deceased. All this additional information is most helpful and saves a great deal of research time.

The first birth, death and marriage certificates, issued in 1855 contained much additional information. The birth certificates give the parents' ages and birthplaces and the number of other siblings living and deceased. The marriage certificates give the places of present residence and the usual residence if different of both bride and groom and details of any previous marriages. The death certificates give the place of birth, details of marriage, burial place and all living and deceased siblings. Sadly, for genealogists and family historians, as the volume of work grew the inclusion of this additional information was not continued after 1855.

Scottish records are held in New Register House, Edinburgh. For an inclusive search fee (see Appendix) the researcher has access to the indexes from 1855 for births, marriages and deaths, and divorces from 1984. Also available are old Parish registers pre-1855 and the census records from 1841 to 1891.

Each researcher is given a numbered seat at a desk. All indexes are on computer and searching is very easy. Instructions for use are given at each terminal and the computer will offer various recorded spellings for each name. There is also a very useful cross check for female marriages and deaths as these are indexed under all known surnames, i.e. maiden surname, previous and present married names.

Original records are not open for inspection but most are available on self service access microfiche or microfilm so you can check you have the correct entry before ordering and paying for copy certificates. You can also get photocopies or make accurate copies without purchasing certificates or photocopies if you prefer. (Remember to cite your sources!) This helps you to continue your researches, making full use of your time at the Registry. For instance, if you find a correct birth certificate this will give you the names and ages of both parents; a marriage certificate will give you the names of both sets of parents. Note this information and return to the indexes to search for the relevant page and volume numbers. One visit could uncover several generations.

When you have found your entry in the computer index,

complete the relevant (colour coded) order form. Take the microfiche or microfilm that you require and replace it with your order form, first detaching the counterfoil on which you should have noted the entry number that you wish to search. You can remove three fiches or two films at a time. After use, put them in the relevant trays for filing. If you require some minor records, fill in an orange order form and put it in a request tray. An attendant will bring the register to your seat number.

The attendants are very knowledgeable; they can often point you in the right direction if the record inspected proves to be the wrong one and will help you to master the equipment.

Before visiting New Register House it is advisable to book your seat in advance by letter or phone. The Registry issue very informative free literature (which can be obtained by post) showing what records they hold, their charges and times of opening, which will help you plan your visit in advance. There are, of course, charges for copy certificates; these are less if you search the indexes yourself but you may find that the assistance of the Registry staff is worth the extra charge. You may only use pencils here; they sell them in aid of a local charity to anyone who forgets to bring one.

A genealogical search room will shortly open in Glasgow. This will be linked by computer to New Register House in Edinburgh and, as there, bookings will have to be made in advance and a search fee will be charged. (See Appendix.)

Ireland

If you go to Dublin, I suggest you visit the Genealogical Office in Kildare Street before you visit the research centres. This offers an excellent consultancy service where for £20/hour a professional genealogist will assist you and give advice on where to search and what is available. An appointment can be made in advance to avoid wasted time.

Civil registration in Ireland commenced in 1864 and the indexes are kept at the Registrar General's office. A charge is made for the privilege of searching the indexes. There is a small comfortable search room with separate tables and all the indexes are housed in that room. There are usually two very helpful clerks on duty.

Birth certificates in Ireland give the date and exact place of birth, the name of the child, the full name, occupation and residence of the father, the maiden name of the mother and the name of the person present at the birth. Marriage certificates give the names of the parties, date and place of the marriage, the place of residence of the bride and groom and the names of their fathers. Death certificates only give the name of the deceased, the age and the date and place of death. The original records are not open to inspection by the public, but once you have found what you think is the correct entry you can pay a lesser fee for a photocopy of the entry. The copy will be brought to you in a short time. Once again you have only spent a small sum to find out and not paid the full fee for a certificate as you would in England and Wales. When you are sure you have the correct entry the full fee can be paid and the certificates ordered and supplied while you wait. It is therefore possible to carry out your searches and obtain your certificates without waiting too long, enabling you to further your searches the same day. The fees payable are in Irish punts, English currency is not accepted in Dublin. If you wish to send a remittance to Ireland, you can obtain a bank draft or Irish currency from most banks. If you send currency, use registered post.

Northern Ireland

All the original registers and records for Northern Ireland which commence with the partition of Ireland in 1922 are kept in the General Register Office, Belfast. The Belfast registry also holds some records for the northern counties of southern Ireland (the counties of Cavan, Monaghan and Donegal). This is because before partition these counties were part of Ulster. Birth certificates will give you the date and place of birth, name, sex; full name, occupation and usual residence of father; maiden name of mother, date of registration and name and residence of informant. Marriage certificates give the date, names and ages of both bride and groom together with their residences at the date of marriage and their occupations, the names of the fathers of the bride and groom and their occupations. Information on death certificates is similar to that given on the English certificates. The Belfast Office have a unique system to assist family history researchers. Appointments have to be made in advance and the office will usually take only one researcher each day. For a comparatively small fee per day, the researcher is given an assistant and 6 hours free range of all original documents held in the registry. One day's searching can give you details of a whole family. There is also a fee for copy certificates. However, if you do not seek copies for your records you can, provided you are meticulous, copy the original documents into your notebook and dispense with copy certificates. Unfortunately, due to staff holidays this registry is normally closed to genealogists during the summer from July to September, an important point to remember. However they will issue copy certificates by mail if requested to do so. The registry will also carry out a one name five year search of their records for a small fee.

The Isle of Man

Here again, if your family originally came from the Isle of Man and even if they moved on around the world which many Manxmen did, all the records are held in close proximity. Compulsory registration commenced in 1878, and all the research can be carried out at the Registry, which is on the first floor of the General Registry building in Douglas. The information available from the certificates is similar to that shown in certificates from England and Wales. There are no search fees and the helpful staff will produce the indexes and also the original registers once you have found the entries you require. Copies of the certificates are obtainable on payment of a fee.

The Channel Islands

If you need to research records in the Channel Islands, civil registration began in 1842 and some of the early documents, particularly pre-20th century, may be written in French. No personal searches of the Jersey registers may be made, but postal enquiries should be addressed to the Librarian at the Société Jersiaise who will charge a search fee. Personal researchers may use the Société's excellent library which contains a wealth of local and genealogical material. None of the records held in Guernsey are open for public research and only postal enquiries are dealt with. Application should be made to the Registrar General in Guernsey for records for Guernsey and the other Channel Islands. A telephone call to the Registry will give you details of the amounts charged for copy certificates and searches.

You will, by now, have realised that all the registries adopt different methods. The least helpful to family historians being the largest at St. Catherine's House.

All the registries will supply copy certificates by mail provided you can give them sufficient information and send the correct fee with your application. In the case of birth certificates they require the full name of the person, the date and place of birth and the name of the parents. The maiden name of the mother is only required for entries after September 1911. For marriage certificates, the date and place, full names of both parties and the names of the fathers if possible. For death certificates, the full name of the deceased, place and date of death. If the person was married the full name of the spouse is also helpful. Charges vary from registry to registry. The Registry at St. Catherine's House issues a leaflet giving the fees and charges for all the other registries, but a telephone call direct to the registry in question will elicit their requirements as to fees and save time and correspondence.

Most registries do not have the facilities for protracted correspondence and are unable to deal with detailed written enquiries. If incorrect applications are made, they will be returned with a printed form stating what is wrong, usually by the method of ticking the various printed options.

Each certificate you obtain will lead you further in your researches. A birth certificate will give you the parents' names, including the mother's maiden name, the address at which they were living, and the father's occupation, enabling you to search the registry indexes for the marriage of the parents, and the census returns for the address which could reveal ages and other family members.

A marriage certificate will give you the names of the fathers of the bride and groom and their occupations, the addresses of both parties, their ages and occupations from which you can search the registry for the birth dates of the bride and groom, and the census for addresses which should give details of their parents such as ages and any others of the families present at the census count.

A death certificate will give you the age, occupation and address of the deceased, the maiden name if a married woman, the name of a spouse and the name and relationship of the informant. This information can lead to a date of birth, a date of death of the spouse if the deceased was a widow or widower and an address for the informant – certainly a point worth following in the Census records.

The more certificates you obtain, the more you will be able to evaluate the information they contain in relation to further research.

4
KEEPING YOUR RECORDS

What is the main objective of the family historian? It is exactly the same as the professional historian. To record the historical events and genealogy of a family, offering the reader a well documented presentation, interesting not only to the historian and his family but to anyone who chooses to read it.

Record keeping is sometimes felt to be the most difficult area of family history research. Family trees often have gaps and no cross references so that clear identification of individual members of the family and their relationships is not possible. Careful methodical recording not only helps you to clarify and direct your own thoughts, but can act as a guide showing where to commence your next searches. It is also an important requisite if your researches are to be of assistance to future researchers. It is important to record both negative and positive searches so that you can remember where you were *unable* to find some piece of information and do not duplicate the work. It also gives direction if you stop at any given point and do not follow up the result of a piece of research. You will know that there is material there to follow up later.

Now that you have amassed a fair amount of material the time has come to decide how you will store and record it and how you should prepare your first family tree. If you have never worked in an office, where filing and collating information are routine, don't be daunted by what may seem to you an endless amount of paper work. While you are recording and sorting all the information you have collected it will begin to fall into some sort of order and you will understand what you are trying to do.

The main points to bear in mind are that you wish to achieve:

1. The recording of all the information gained, in a system giving easy access to that information.
2. The safe storage of original documents in a system easily displayed.
3. The preparation of a simple easily followed family tree.

A visit to any office stationer will give you some idea of the many methods of storage and information recording now available. Rigid plastic boxes and card index cabinets, folders, box, concertina and pocket files, plastic document holders and display envelopes, loose flat files and photograph albums. The possibilities are many and varied. The cost varies widely also, therefore a great deal should not be spent until you discover the method which you find easiest and which will fit into the space you have available.

Recording the Information
How are you going to keep your records? Chronologically (date order) or by name? The answer is both, by using a system of cross references. The easiest method is to use a card index system which can also be colour coded, using the same colour cards for each family which will make it even easier for quick access. For your main family (probably your father's surname) the cards can be white, for your next family (probably your mother's family surname) the cards can be blue. You can use any colour combination you choose. If you prefer to use only one colour of card you can use a system with coloured marking pens, highlighting connecting members of one family by

drawing a line through the names, using a different colour for each family.

Cards, ruled or plain, together with plain and indexed guide cards in various colours to be inserted between the groups can be purchased in several sizes and you will soon discover the best size for you. Rigid plastic boxes with hinged lids, which hold approximately 1000 cards, to fit the various sizes of cards are readily available, as are larger index cabinets with movable divisions. If you are going to adopt the card colour coding system, a card box for each colour might prove the best method with which to begin. If you are using the marker system, one large cabinet with colour coded divisions could be used. It is essential that all boxes and files be clearly labelled showing the contents.

If you do not wish to commit yourself to a particular card size when you first start your records, clear plastic food boxes with different coloured lids in many sizes are available and are less expensive than the custom made boxes. They can be used quite effectively to store your card index system. Even more economical is the use of strong cardboard boxes with lids. If you wonder why I emphasise that your storage boxes should have lids, the reason is that paper seems to gather dust wherever it is stored. While over the years your cards may look a little dog-eared from constant usage, if they are kept in covered containers they will keep cleaner and will not have to be renewed so often.

As you sort, evaluate and record the information you have gathered, you will need somewhere to keep the original notes you have made. These can be kept in box files, one box to each family, the notes kept in either alphabetically indexed sections or simply in chronological order inside the box. Alternatively, they can be kept in concertina files or individual pocket or wallet files. The pocket or wallet files which can be purchased in different colours to match your colour codes and are reasonably priced may be the best when starting.

When you have decided on the card size and method you are going to use, as an exercise, start with yourself and record all the information that you have. In order to save time and space, there are standard genealogical abbreviations for frequently used words which are used universally as follows:

b.	*born*	div.	*divorced*
bapt.	*baptised*	dau.	*daughter*
bur.	*buried*	unm.	*unmarried*
d.	*died*	=	*married*
m.	*male*	f.	*female*

Two other words frequently used in genealogy are "spouse" meaning marriage partner either male or female and "siblings" meaning brothers and sisters in the same family.

Always write the dates in full; do not use abbreviations or numbers for the months. Abbreviations for January, June and July (Jan., Jun., Jul.) can be confusing, and September has not always been the ninth month. Dates should be recorded with the day first followed by the month and the year – 27th January 1899.

Using your white cards, or whatever colour you have chosen for your family name, begin by recording the name cards with the following information on one card:

Top line	– capital letters	your name
second line	– b. (for born)	date of birth
third line	– at	place of birth
fourth line	– married	date of marriage
fifth line	– at	place of marriage
sixth line	– father	name of father
seventh line	– mother	maiden name of mother

If you are unmarried put "unm" beside your name and don't include the lines referring to the date and place of marriage.

If you are married, continue:

eighth line	– spouse	name of husband/wife
ninth line	– children	names and sex of children

Beside your name in the top right hand corner of the card put your reference number "W1" (1 for the first name to be recorded and "W" for white). If you use only white cards your reference should show the colour of marker used for each family, i.e. R1 (red) B1 (blue) G1 (green) etc. If you have family names that you intend to follow at a later date you could give them the reference "M" for miscellaneous and need not give them a colour. Additional information such as when and where baptised can be included on the back of the card. You can also record a note of where your copy birth certificate and any other documents are held. It may be necessary, as you gather more information, to use more than one card for each person, but provided you use your reference numbers and file all the cards for one person together this will prove no problem.

From this information you can prepare more white cards. Your father:

Top line	– capital letters	his full name	"W2"
second line	– b.	date of birth	
third line	– at	place of birth	
fourth line	– married	date of marriage	
fifth line	– at	place of marriage	
sixth line	– father	father's full name	
seventh line	– mother	mother's name	

eighth line – spouse   maiden name of wife
ninth line   – children   names and sex of children

Your own name as connecting link will appear on the ninth line and you can put the number "W1" beside it to show where further information can be obtained concerning yourself.

As you proceed making and numbering cards you can put the references beside all the connecting names. Put as much information as you have on each card. As more information comes to light the cards can be updated. As you go further back in time, you might enter on the back of the cards a note of where the information was obtained. As emphasised in previous chapters it is essential to cite your sources of information. When you have had some practice of record making you will be able to decide what information you wish to include on each card, but a general rule is to record as much as you know about each person. Cards should be kept for each individual encountered.

The following illustrations are a set of name cards for my own family which I started many years ago as a beginner, only the surnames are changed (Figures 5 and 6). I have remained faithful to this system of recording which I find gives quick and easy access to all available information. From these samples you will see how the reference numbers at the top of each card appear on other cards so that you will have easy access to any person by referring to the numbers and finding the cards. You will also see the reason for numbering each person recorded. In many families male children are named after fathers or grandfathers and female children after grandmothers or favourite aunts. Some families have a tradition of giving the firstborn son the same name through the generations and Scots families sometimes give a son his mother's family

```
SMITH, LESLIE GEORGE                        W1

b.          1 January 1923
at          County Borough of West Ham
married     27 March 1949
at          County Borough of West Ham
father      SMITH, CHARLES WILLIAM (W2)
mother      ROBERTS, JEANNIE REBECCA (R1)
spouse      CARTER, ESTHER (B1)
children    Anthony (W13), Susan (W14)
```

(a)

```
Occupation - Link Man, Royal Opera House,
                Covent Garden

Served British Navy (Chief Petty Officer)
    1940 - 1945



Birth & Marriage Certificates, Navy Discharge
    Papers, Photographs (Book 2)
```

(b)

Fig. 5 (a) Front of index card for Leslie George Smith
          (b) Back of index card for Leslie George Smith

name as a first name. So, unless there is a clear identification of each name, the records could soon become muddled and difficult to follow.

If you are using a separate box for each family, the cards can be filed numerically, using the reference numbers. Alternatively if you are using one box for all your cards you can file the cards alphabetically by surname. As a cross reference a set of cards can be prepared on a

```
SMITH, GEORGE WILLIAM JOSEPH        W3

b.          23 April 1878
at          Dartford, Kent
married      19 November 1898
at          Dartford, Kent
d.          25 December 1939
at          Dartford
father      SMITH, WILLIAM CHARLES (W4)
mother      DEAN, SARAH ANN (M6)
spouse      SHARPE, EMMA JANE (M5)
children    Susan (W7), Eliza (W8),
            Charles William (W2),
            Ann Sophia Dean (W9)
```

(a)

```
Occupation - Journeyman

Lived Mount Pleasant House, Dartford,
   Kent all his life

Bapt. St. Mark's Church, Dartford, Kent


Birth, Death & Marriage Certificates
   (Book 1)
```

(b)

Fig. 6 (a) Front of index card for George William Joseph
Smith
(b) Back of index card for George William Joseph
Smith

chronological basis, filed in date order. These will not require reference numbers, but will, of course, show the reference numbers of each person beside the names. Samples of these cards are also given (Figure 7).

These index cards are for your own use and will form

```
1922

24 June    Married

           SMITH, CHARLES WILLIAM (W2)
           ROBERTS, JEANNIE REBECCA (R1)
```

(a)

```
1878

23 April  b.    SMITH, GEORGE WILLIAM
                         JOSEPH (W3)
```

(b)

Fig. 7 (a) Chronological index card for 1922
      (b) Chronological index card for 1878

the basis of the information shown on your family trees and in your written history. If you are asked how you know that a distant relative was deported to Australia for stealing a loaf of bread, your index cards will tell you where you obtained the information and where any documentation is stored.

It is important at this stage to start a general information and address book or card index. The book can be a loose leaf ring binder with two sections, one divided alphabetically for addresses. Or you can continue to use a card index system. Enter in alphabetical order every address you need and even those you think you may not need again; relatives, registries, records offices and archives, bookshops, family history societies, parish councils and cemeteries. I recently received a letter from an unknown person in Australia seeking my help in tracing a document. He had been given my address by someone I met at a genealogical conference many months ago. My address, taken by someone I would probably never meet again, had proved useful to her. Genealogists and family historians are inveterate note takers, hoarding any snippets of information like squirrels hoarding nuts for the winter!

Any other information such as opening times of libraries, the cost of documents, where to buy certain items, can be entered in the general information section. You will soon learn to distinguish what sort of information will be helpful and which you wish to record.

At this stage of preparing your family history patience and meticulous attention to detail are required. If record making appears a tedious exercise at first, persevere. It will soon become second nature and you will enjoy completing your cards, adding information as it is obtained. Your diligence will also be rewarded when after several years' work you are still able to return to your first notes and find information without difficulty.

Storing Original Documents

Copy birth, death and marriage certificates, original letters, photocopies, photographs and precious elderly papers need to be stored so that they do not suffer damage but can be easily displayed for they will play a major supporting role when you show your family history. Once again a visit to a stationery suppliers will enable you to evaluate the various methods available. Books of clear plastic pockets are available in many sizes and with a range in the number of pockets they contain. The covers, usually with an outside pocket for a label, come in several colours and can be used to fit in with your colour coding. Where documents such as certificates need to be read on only one side, two can be placed back to back in one pocket. Letters, if written on two sides of a page, can easily be read. The plastic pockets can be turned like the pages of a book and will protect the documents. An index of contents can be placed in a pocket provided on the inside cover or in the first pocket if preferred. These documents can be filed chronologically, starting with the present day and working backwards or with the earliest documents you have and working forwards to the present day.

For each person you may have a birth, marriage and death certificate, a baptismal certificate and several other documents. A photocopy of a bible entry, newspaper items referring to a 21st birthday celebration, giving the names of those present (very useful if you are able to make the family connections). Keep all the documents relating to one person together placing them in the pockets in chronological order, thus building a picture of their life and times. It is these certificates and documents which will put the meat on the bones of your family history and bring the people to life. The reference numbers and colour codes can be used in the index to link the documentation with the information cards. The following illustrations are sample index/contents pages showing the documents which can be

CONTENTS

1. Fragments of history – The Smith Family (author unknown)
2. Handwritten Parliamentary Return – Smith family with initialled note "DS 1815"
3. Memorandum handwritten by William Charles Smith 1867 with handwritten family history
4. Receipt 1900 – William Charles Smith
5. Letter 1878 – Sarah Ann Dean
6. Copy Memorandum – handwritten by William Smith
7. Extract from Charles William Smith's Manuscript Book
8. Handwritten note re Smith of Dartford (author unknown)
9. Smith family tree – letter E. Smith (undated)
10. Handwritten notes re Smith family (author unknown)
11. Handwritten Smith Family Tree (author unknown)
12. Letter 1894 – Jessie Smith
13. Letter 1894 – Rev. R. S. Graves
14. Smith place names with note Rev. R. S. Graves
15. Handwritten note re Smith family (author unknown)
16. Handwritten note re Smith family 1907
17. Letter 1912 – Frederick Appleton
18. Handwritten copy of The Parish Registers of Dartford made by Charles Smith of Barringdon Street
19. Letter Margaret F. Smith
20. Drawing Smith family crest (artist unknown)

Fig. 8. Example contents page for plastic pockets

CONTENTS

1. Census Return – Dartford District 1851.
2. Census Record – West Ham 1871.
3. Marriage Certificate – William Charles Smith (W4)/ Sarah Ann Dean (M6)
4. Death Certificate – William Charles Smith (W4)
5. Copy Will and Grant of Probate – William Charles Smith (W4)
6. Birth Certificate – Samuel Charles Smith (W5)
7. Death Certificate – Samuel Charles Smith (W5)
8. Marriage Certificate – George William Joseph Smith (W3)/Emma Jane Sharpe (M5)
9. Copy Will and Grant of Probate – George William Joseph Smith (W3)
10. Copy Will and Grant of Probate – Emma Jane Smith née Sharpe (M5)
11. Marriage Certificate – William Smith (W6)/Ann Perkins (M8)
12. Marriage Certificate – George Henry Roberts (R2)/ Sarah Jane Dowsett (M1)
13. Birth Certificate – Charles William Smith (W2)
14. Photographs – 6 Constance Street, Silvertown, West Ham (W2)
15. Photographs – Mount Pleasant House, Dartford (W3)
16. Photograph – Wedding: Charles William Smith (W2)/ Jeannie Rebecca Roberts (R1)
17. Photographs – Burial plot showing memorial column and enclosure rails, Highgate Cemetery: Samuel Charles Smith (W5), George William Joseph Smith (W3), Emma Jane Smith née Sharpe (M5), Susan Smith (W7) and Eliza Smith (W8)
18. Map and booklet – Highgate Cemetery
19. Photocopy – pages 'Past and Present' relating to West Ham

Fig. 9. Example index page. This one shows cross-references to index cards

displayed (Figures 8 and 9). The information where the documents are stored can be entered on the index cards as a cross reference.

Photographs can be kept in conventional photograph albums or the new type of album with loose leaf pages each with its own clear plastic cover. The photographs are placed on the stiff pages under the covers and are easily moved and changed round. Each photograph should be clearly identified. If of a person, the individual should be named and their reference number shown. If a photograph of a house or a monumental inscription, details should be given and a reference number of the person to whom the picture relates. Photographs can be kept in the folders with other information if preferred. A plastic pocket will hold several photographs. Details can be written on a piece of card inserted in the pocket. A small piece of double sided sticky tape or a tiny spot of 'Blu-tack' will hold the pictures in position, but they will be movable when required. If a card slightly smaller in size than the pocket is used this will give support to flimsy photographs. Photographs and information can be placed on each side of the card, making the most economic use of a plastic pocket.

A computer or word processor can be a great help in keeping and collating your records – you can keep a great amount of information on 1 or 2 disks. It is possible to buy genealogical programs, some of which are very comprehensive and will enable you to prepare and print family trees and charts. Others will collate family relationships, ages, birth and death dates and index source material, etc. Some very sophisticated programs will even allow you to add photographs. Information relating to computer programs and their uses is given in some family history books and magazines. The Family Tree Magazine devotes a whole part of each month's issue to the use of computers and programs.

5

YOUR FIRST FAMILY TREE

Preparing your first family tree from the information you have gathered requires patience and experiment. It will probably be necessary to try several drafts before deciding on the size, style and shape you wish to adopt. The amount of detail recorded will be up to you and will depend upon the depth of your researches, but a simple family tree will be helpful and will encourage you to go on with the work.

It is rare for a family tree to be complete in every detail; too many individuals appear without full information. Relationships are not always clearly defined, but if your tree is based upon the information contained in your card index, with the reference numbers shown by each name, missing information can be checked from time to time and when obtained added to the chart and the card. It is important to include the reference numbers since if you prepare a chart for each family name you will then have a cross reference to show where the family relationships lie between the families by referring to the numbers given to each person.

It is impossible even to contemplate recording every name on a single chart. I have known a researcher use a roll of wallpaper, but even that gave insufficient room and was very difficult to read since it meant rolling it up from one end until the name required was reached and the rolled ends kept snapping together if they were not held strongly apart.

How and where you store the charts will play a part in deciding the size. They can be stored flat in a drawer or rolled and held by elastic bands. Rolling the charts gives more storage room, but makes it necessary to pin them out on a board for easy reading. A chart for each family could be prepared on size A3 (17″ × 12″/43cm × 30cm) paper and a display book with plastic pockets used. The charts could be placed back to back with thin card between to support them, two in each pocket so that a book of 20 pockets could hold 40 charts. The charts could be shown chronologically commencing either with the earliest known name or your own name. This is the display and storage system I use myself. The final family tree (following only your paternal line) might be framed and hung in a prominent position in your house. It could be hand written for you by a calligrapher in special lettering with names in different colours and line drawings of associated houses or places.

It is possible to purchase printed family charts in many sizes, some fanciful and some plain, coloured or black and white. The Society of Genealogists offers a choice of several as do the Federation of Family History Societies. Genealogical magazines contain advertisements for many different styles of chart. A chart with a printed tree – usually an oak – with the main family name on the trunk of the tree and spaces for names on the branches. A large circle with a space in the middle for the main name and segments for each family radiating outwards. The choices are many and varied as is the cost. If you join your local Family History Society or visit the Society of Genealogists you will, no doubt, see the charts prepared by other members which may help you to decide on your final size and design.

Your first family tree or chart should, however, be a simple record of your findings, using the abbreviations given previously and should concentrate on one family only. As you progress, further charts can be prepared for each family with the reference numbers showing the links between the families. It is easiest at this stage to start with the present day and work back into the past although you may elect in your final chart to start with the first known person of the family and work forwards to the present day.

A reasonable size sheet on which to draft your first chart is 17″ × 12″ (43cm × 30cm). This should give you ample room to display four generations. Paper this size and in varying qualities can be purchased from stationery suppliers and is known as size "A3". An alternative size is 13″ × 8″ (33cm × 20cm) known as "foolscap". Lay the paper in front of you with the longest side at the top and the shorter side running vertically from top to bottom. Arm yourself with pencils, a 12″ (30cm) rule and an eraser. It is preferable not to use biro or permanent ink when first drafting your chart. It is easy to go over the pencil work with ink when you are satisfied with your first efforts. Before starting, rough in the blocks where you think the names will come on the paper in order not to waste too many sheets on your drafts.

The following measurements are based on using the size A3 paper. Begin by blocking in the areas where the information is to be written. Against the left side of the paper, 5″ (127mm) down from the top draw a horizontal line 3½″ (89mm) long. Two inches (50mm) below that another horizontal line 3½″ (89mm) long. Against the right hand edge of these lines, 3½″ (89mm) down from the top of the page draw a vertical line 5″ (127mm) long with horizontal lines of 3½″ (89mm) each at the top and bottom. This will give three areas where your own name and those of your parents will be written. Follow across the page in a similar manner, dividing each area created by two. When you reach the right hand side of the page you will have four blocks

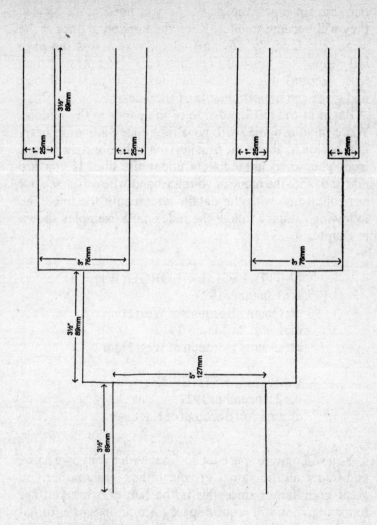

Fig 10. Dimensions for the family tree outline

marked out down the page. As you need more blocks, they will become smaller. Keep the horizontal lines at the same length of 3½" (89mm) all the way across the page but reduce the vertical lines first to 3" (76mm) and then to 1" (25mm). Figure 10 shows how your page will look and gives the measurements of the lines.

Begin at the left hand side of the paper in the middle. Write in your name, with your reference number in brackets beside it, above the first horizontal line and the details from your card immediately under the line. If you are married write the name of your husband/wife on the second horizontal line with the details underneath the line. The following samples follow the index card examples shown in chapter 4.

SMITH, LESLIE GEORGE (W1)
b.: 1 January 1923
at: County Borough of West Ham
married: 24 March 1949
at: County Borough of West Ham

CARTER, ESTHER (B1)
b.: 2 November 1927
at: London Borough of Hackney

You will require space for six lines under your own name and under all the names of your father, grandfather and great grandfather since this is the family name you are following. You will require space for four lines of information beneath the other names. Move across the page to the right and put your father's name on the next top horizontal line with his details under that line. Move down the page to the next horizontal line and put in your mother's name with her details under the line.

SMITH, CHARLES WILLIAM (W2)
b.: 1 August 1900
at: Dartford, Kent
father   married: 24 June 1922
at: West Ham, Essex
d.: 15 May 1972
at: London Borough of Newham

ROBERTS, JEANNIE REBECCA (R1)
b.: 23 April 1899
mother   at: County Borough of West Ham
d.: 4 February 1975
at: London Borough of Newham

Now you have two generations of your paternal line on paper, follow through across the page using the same method of horizontal and vertical lines to guide you. Add the third generation, your grandparents, and the fourth generation, your great grandparents. The second main line will show your maternal grandparents and great grandparents.

If you have roughed out the blocks first you should find that the measurements given fit the paper size. If you use different sized paper you may find that you have left insufficient room to accommodate all the names and need to start several drafts until you reach a satisfactory result. Figure 11 shows how your chart should look, with the names, references and details clearly shown. If there is information missing, you can put a question mark to denote that fact. If you wish to remind yourself of missing information that is to be researched you can mark the space with a small coloured sticky spot which can be removed when the information is inserted. These coloured spots can be purchased in packets in most stationers. In order to avoid confusion, I usually use small gold spots, a colour

SMITH, CHARLES WILLIAM (W2)

b.: 1 August 1900
at: Dartford, Kent
married: 24 June 1922
at: West Ham, Essex
d.: 15 May 1972
at: London Borough of Newham

SMITH, LESLIE GEORGE (W1)

b.: 1 January 1923
at: County Borough of West Ham
married: 27 March 1949
at: County Borough of West Ham

CARTER, ESTHER (B1)

b.: 2 November 1927
at: London Borough of Hackney

ROBERTS, JEANNIE REBECCA (R1)

b.: 23 April 1899
at: County Borough of West Ham
d.: 4 February 1975
at: London Borough of Newham

Fig 11. Sample Family Tree.

SMITH, WILLIAM CHARLES (W4)

b.: 1847
at: Dartford, Kent
married: 27 May 1876
at: Dartford, Kent
d.: 8 July 1907
at: Dartford

SMITH,
GEORGE WILLIAM JOSEPH (W3)

b.: 23 April 1878
at: Dartford, Kent
married: 19 November 1898
at: Dartford
d.: 25 December 1939
at: Dartford

DEAN, SARAH ANN (M6)

b.: 1850
at: Calcutta, India
d.: 1900

SHARPE, FRANK WILLIAM (M7)

b.: 1830
at: Dartford, Kent
married: ?
at: ?
d.: ?
at: ?

SHARPE, EMMA JANE (M5)

b.: 5 January 1879
at: Dartford, Kent
d.: 21 August 1950
at: Dartford

ROBERTS, CORNELIUS (R3)

b.: 1847
at: Ireland
married: ?
at: ?
d.: ?

ROBERTS, GEORGE HENRY (R2)

b.: 17 October 1872
at: Co. Clare, Ireland
married: 8 October 1894
at: Bow Common, London
d.: 6 January 1938
at: Leyton, Essex

BROWN, ELIZABETH (M4)

b.: 1846
at: West Ham, Essex
d.: ?

DOWSETT, SAMUEL (M2)

b.: 1838
at: Halstead, Essex
married: 29 June 1860
at: Braintree, Essex
d.: 1 October 1878
at: Halstead

DOWSETT, SARAH JANE (M1)

b.: 9 September 1867
at: Braintree, Essex
d.: ?

different from any of my family reference colours.

Looking at the chart you will see that although you wish to keep the chart to one family name, other names have been included, but the main family name being followed is always at the top of the page. You can then prepare similar charts using the same method for any other families researched. Although you will probably concentrate on one name when you start, information about other connected families will be gathered so that family charts can be started for each connecting family and completed as the information comes to light. Probably the next chart will concentrate on your mother's family name. Once started, most family researchers do not concentrate solely on their paternal line, nor try to research all their ancestors, but follow a few of the families as the intertwining details are gathered. Turning to the sample chart in Figure 11 you will see that you can learn quite a lot of information about the male lines of the Smith and Roberts families, that three generations of Smiths were born in Dartford in Kent and the Roberts family originated in Ireland, where they married and died, but little about their spouses and nothing about any other siblings.

If you wish to prepare a chart showing more detail of one family only, it is necessary to commence with the oldest known name. If you use this method, brothers and sisters, not shown on the previous chart can be shown. Using the same size sheet of paper – A3 – start by putting the name in the centre at the top of the page. The following chart can be prepared commencing with the great grandfather shown as the last entry on the previous chart. Write in the name and details as follows;

SMITH, WILLIAM   =   DEAN, SARAH ANN
CHARLES (W4)   (M6)
     1847–1907   1850–1900

Draw a short vertical line from the middle under the equals (married) sign then a horizontal line at the bottom of the vertical line. You can then show all the children of William Charles and Sarah Ann Dean by drawing short

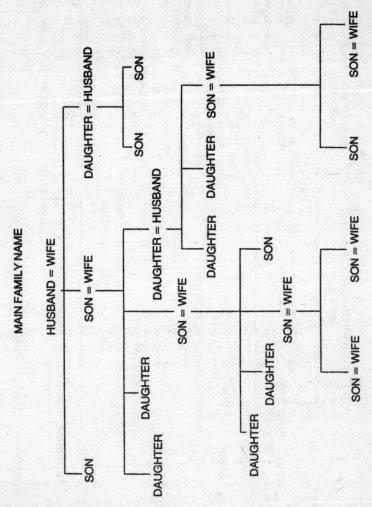

Fig. 12. Grid without names but showing relationships.

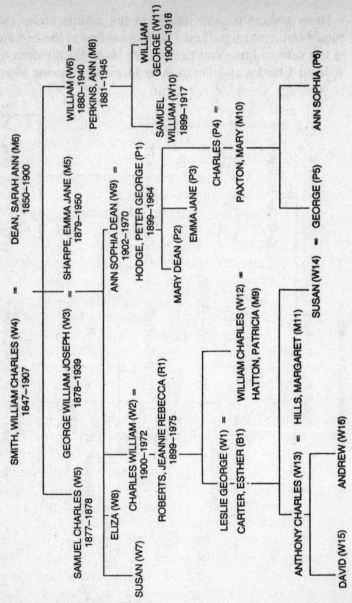

Fig. 13. Smith Family Tree.

vertical lines down from the horizontal line and inserting their names, dates of birth and death, starting with the eldest on the left hand side. If they married you can also show the names of their partners. Figure 12 shows a grid without the names but with the relationships. Follow the male lines which will always have the same family name. The children shown on the second horizontal line will be the second generation and those on the third horizontal line will be the third generation. Brothers and sisters of each generation will be shown and their children will be cousins. The names on the fourth generation will be the great grandchildren of the first name at the top of the page. Details of the female line may be entered, but not followed if there is insufficient room on the page. If you wish you can highlight your own line through the chart by using a different colour to write the names and the actual lines drawn from one generation to the next. It is quite difficult to plan this style of family tree to fit the space available, particularly if you wish to show as many of the family as possible. This could include brothers, sisters, uncles, aunts and cousins all belonging to the same family and is a chart which concentrates more particularly on one family name than the previous style of chart shown. Drafting this form of chart will take careful planning, using long and short vertical and horizontal lines to make best use of the space. Figure 13 shows a family tree prepared in this form. It is the form of family tree most often used for families with very well documented histories such as a branch of a royal family but once you have decided at which point to stop your research on your own family name, it may be the style of chart you wish to have handwritten and framed.

Reading Figure 13, what can you learn about the Smith family? The first known Smith was William Charles born in 1847 who married Sarah Ann Dean. They had three children. Samuel Charles, George William Joseph and William. (The name William appears throughout this family, with the two brothers George William and William presumably being named after their father. In the past, it was not unusual for parents to name a child after a deceased child who had died at a very early age. Sometimes the same name was given to several children of the same parents until one survived.)

George William Joseph, whose line we are following, married Emma Jane Sharpe and they had four children. Susan and Eliza have no birth or death dates. Checking with their index cards, we find that neither lived longer than a few weeks. Charles William married Jeannie Rebecca Roberts and they had two children one of whom was Leslie George (our researcher) who has also included his own spouse, Esther Carter, and his children, Anthony and Susan. Anthony's children are also shown, bringing us up to the present day and showing six generations of the Smith family.

The third child of William Charles and Sarah Ann was William who married Ann Perkins. Two children were born of that marriage, Samuel William and William George. Both Samuel William and William George died young leaving no issue, so that line of the Smith family died out. Looking at the dates of death of Samuel William and William George it would be reasonable to assume that they both died in the 1914–1918 war. This information would be shown on their index cards or in original or copy documentation.

Ann Sophia Dean Smith, daughter of George William Joseph and Emma Jane, sister of Charles William, married Peter Hodge and the family line of Hodge is followed. The reason for the inclusion of this new family name becomes clear when Ann Sophia Dean's grandson, George Hodge, marries Susan Smith, the granddaughter of her brother Charles William, thus bringing two branches of the Smith family together again.

Both forms of family tree, Figures 11 and 13, give information about the Smith family and are complementary. They can be filed in a display book facing each other in two of the plastic pockets so that they can be read in conjunction showing a substantial amount of the history of the Smith family. (If you are using a genealogical program on a computer, this will prepare a family tree for you.)

This short analysis of the Smith Family Tree shows how much we know about the family. When we have even more detailed information we can proceed to the writing of the history using our index cards, notes and family tree to guide us.

6
WHERE DO WE GO FROM HERE?

Most beginners are able to find their own birth certificates and those of their parents, but what do you do if you are unable to get any further? If you cannot obtain the certificates you need to start you on your trail, what do you do?

Using your own birth certificate as a sample, go back to the beginning to look for clues and try to find your parents' marriage. If one of your parents had an uncommon surname, look for that name first since you will have less searching to do. If both have a fairly common name like Smith or Jones, concentrate on your father's name first. Usually your parents were married some time before your birth date – but not necessarily so. When you look into your family history, be prepared to learn many things you did not know – and for some shocks. You may unearth some family skeletons but your curiosity is natural and tracking a family history can reveal that some of our ancestors lived different or eccentric lives. How brave they were and worthy of admiration when they defied convention in a day and age when social behaviour which we now take for granted was considered outrageous and a scandal. You also have to take into account that registration may have taken place at a later date or in a different place.

Starting one year before your birth look for your father's name in the marriage indexes, systematically searching the indexes back from that date. When searching the indexes in this way, prepare your notes carefully so that you do

not miss any volumes. Write the names of the parties to
the marriage at the top of a page in your notebook. Underneath the names write the dates of each year, one line for
each year. Underneath each year write the quarters and
the books in each quarter. As you search, cross off each
volume in turn. You only need look in the particular index
which includes the first letter of the name of the person
you are looking for; for example, if the name was Smith
you would not look in A/K or L/R. In this way you will
not make a mistake and miss one volume, easily done
when you might be searching through ten years, giving at
least 40 volumes and probably 50 or 60 to search. You will
become quite practised and fairly quick. However, be
thorough, don't be tempted to skip through too quickly
causing you to miss the vital names. The following illustration shows how to keep a note of your searches, following
only five years of which four years have been searched:

Smith, William Charles = Dean, Sarah Ann
Smith, William Charles

1873
March	June	September	December
A/K L/R S/Z	A/Z	A/L M/Z	A/Z

1874
March	June	September	December
A/Z	A/K L/Z	A/R S/Z	A/M N/Z

1875
March	June	September	December
A/Z	A/Z	A/Z	A/Z

1876
March	June	September	December
A/R S/Z	A/Z	A/G H/Z	A/K L/Z

1877

March	June	September	December
A/Z	A/K L/R S/Z	A/Z	A/R S/Z

(The ones crossed out are the ones which have been looked at.)

The first time you try this form of searching you may feel frustrated and tempted to give up but the more you carry out these searches the easier it will become.

When you find what you consider to be the correct entry, remember with marriages that you can cross check by looking for the marriage partner. If the volume and page are the same you have found the correct entry. The indexes from 1912 onwards give the name of the marriage partner in brackets which will give you an instant cross check.

If you are unable to find your father's name in your searches, look for your mother's name. In all cases make sure that you have the correct spelling and the correct first names. Many people are known in their family by names which are not the names under which they were registered. It can be quite surprising to learn that your mother who was always referred to as 'Cissie' by your father appears on her birth certificate as Alice Jane. If your father gave the information at the registration of your birth he may have given 'Cissie' as her name. If you have brothers or sisters and you know their dates of birth get a copy of their birth certificates and compare them with your own. They may show slight differences in spellings or names. Look to see who was the informant of the birth. If it was your mother on one of the certificates, her name is more likely to be correct on that one.

If a person had two first names such as Henry George but preferred the second, he may never have used his first name and always called himself George. He may have given the name by which he was known on his marriage certificate which could be different from that on his birth certificate. This did not invalidate the marriage. If they were married and the marriage registered, the marriage was valid even if they used a different name. Ages are often incorrect on marriage certificates, particularly if there was a marked difference in the age of the bride and groom or if the bride was under age and married without the consent of her parents.

If you are unable to find the marriage entry, consider other questions. Were they married overseas or even at sea? If so search the Miscellaneous Indexes, or Marriages at Sea. The Army records can also be a possible area for search. If no marriage can be found, be prepared for the fact that there never was a marriage to be registered and turn your search in another direction.

If you are looking for a birth entry consider the following questions: Are you looking in the right quarter or even the right year? Once again systematic searching, over a period of years either side of the year you think it is, might well be necessary. It is possible for several reasons that the baby was registered in the maiden name of the mother. If a first name had not been decided upon when registration took place the child would have been registered as "male Smith" or "female Smith" and would appear at the end of the entries for Smith. Don't forget the Miscellaneous indexes for babies born abroad. Many births in the early years of compulsory registration were not in fact registered so be prepared for that fact and search elsewhere.

There are also very often mistakes on death certificates since the informant may be a distant relative or a friend giving the information from hearsay. Check the information you have against all the other notes you have made concerning that person. If a widow remarries, the name on her death certificate will be her new surname. Once again don't forget the Miscellaneous indexes for deaths abroad and deaths at sea.

Even with an uncommon surname it is possible to find more than one entry coupled with the same first name. If you find an entry with the name you are looking for, continue your search in case there is a similar name in the same period. If you find a number of entries with the same name and you are not certain which one is 'yours' you can apply to have each name checked against the particulars you have supplied. If you are looking for the birth of Charles Smith you may give as many 'checking points' as you can. His parents' names, George William Smith and Emma Jane Sharpe, the date of birth, the place of birth as exactly as possible, and the occupation of the father. The registry will then, for a fee per name, compare each index reference you give against the checking points given. The form on which to request this search is on the reverse of the application forms for birth, marriage and death certificates. The form asks you to state also whether you wish the registry to stop at the first entry which agrees with your 'checking points' or whether they should continue checking every index reference you have given them. Checking fees are payable for each item checked, whether the search is successful or not. A fee is also payable for the certificate if it is issued. If no certificate is issued, only the checking fees are charged. An information sheet relating to checking is available. The number of this form is CAS/Ref.

Other points to consider if you are unable to trace your missing relative are that the copy certificate you have received from St. Catherine's House on which you are basing your search has been incorrectly copied from the original register. A name badly written in the original register could easily be misread by the person preparing the copy you have received. A name like "Joan Crook" could easily be transcribed as 'Jane Cook'. The original registrar might have misheard what was said at the time of registration. All these things, some of them working together, can be very confusing for the family historian, but must be taken into account when a 'lost' relative cannot be found. If you are relying on addresses shown on the certificate as confirmation, 'Hart Street' could easily become 'Hurd Street'.

The original birth and death registers are held by local registrars and it is possible to search at these local registries. You might find it easier to do this since you will not have to travel so far and you may have several members of one family in the same area. It is advisable to enquire by telephone whether it is necessary to make an appointment and whether you need to book a microfilm machine. Local registries also have different times of opening and closing. A telephone call will help to avoid a wasted journey. Local registrars do make a charge for searching their indexes. Most marriage registers, if the marriage took place in a church after 1837 are still held by the present incumbent of that church, or have been transferred to a local Records Office. An enquiry at the church would give the information as to where the original registers are now kept. Registers of civil marriages and marriages other than the Church of England are held by the local registrar.

If you search the original registers and find that a mistake has been made by the person copying that register and you have an incorrect copy certificate, you can return that copy to St. Catherine's House, pointing out the error and requesting a correct copy. However, if an incorrect entry is made in a register, whether it is a spelling error, an incorrect name or age, or even sex, there is no provision in law for the entry to be corrected, it can never be altered. If a male child is inadvertently entered as female, in the eyes of the law he is female for ever. The registrar might be persuaded to make a note in the margin of the register that an error has occurred, but this would not be shown on any copy certificates issued. If you have any doubts about spellings, ages and names, ask in the family and check the notes you have made from the information you have gathered. It is possible to have several different spellings of a family surname over the generations, in which case other information is necessary to back up your view that the person included in your family history is entitled to be there.

Remember that everybody makes mistakes. Registrars, clerks and officials are no exception. They did and still do make mistakes. If you think you have found one, write to the local registrar or person responsible. Be polite but persistent, do not blame anyone, simply point out the error. If you cannot get a satisfactory answer, try further up the line of responsibility or ask for an interview to explain what you have found. You may be able to get the matter put right, or, if not, an acknowledgement in writing that a mistake has been made which you can use to support your own findings in your records.

If you are unable to proceed with your family history because you really cannot find a way through to the next generation, seek professional help. It is not always as expensive as you might think and a little help is always welcome. There are many professional genealogists and researchers, as in all professions, some good and some bad. Your local County Records Office will have a list of names and your local Family History Society may be able to help. Many advertise in genealogical magazines and there is an Association of Genealogists and Record Agents who have strict requirements for membership. In all cases ask for a list of their fees and charges. Most charge by the hour for work done plus expenses. If you decide to employ a professional agree a limit to the amount you wish to spend requesting that when that limit is reached they do no more work without consulting you. As an example of using professional help, if you wish to obtain some certificates from St. Catherine's House without making a visit or paying their high fees charged for a search, a professional searcher given the names and dates will search the index and obtain a certificate for you. You will have to pay the normal cost of the certificate plus postage and for the time taken. Very often this is less costly than writing to St. Catherine's House direct, particularly if you require several certificates at the same time, and it is almost certainly quicker. Another way a professional can help to save time is by collecting certificates that you have yourself ordered when at the registry, but which you cannot return to collect two days later. Most professional researchers visit St. Catherine's House regularly and could for a small fee collect the certificates and mail them on to you, so that you do not have to wait the two or three weeks taken by the registry to mail certificates to you.

It is difficult to recommend a professional researcher since one person may find a researcher particularly helpful and another experience difficulties with the same person. However, I have listed several researchers in the Appendix to this book who I have found consistently careful and reliable. I take no responsibility if you choose to use their services but hope you will not be disappointed.

7

CENSUS RETURNS

The Census was basically a head count of every person living in England and Wales, Scotland, Northern Ireland, the Channel Islands and the Isle of Man on a certain day and was taken every ten years (except in 1941 during the Second World War) commencing in 1841. In addition to the names and ages of each person, other information was requested which makes the Census Returns one of the most important sources of information for the family history researcher. The Census was compulsory, every house was visited and every person documented from the babies one day old to the oldest in the land, giving a wealth of material for research.

The returns are released to the public after a hundred years. At present the years available to the public for research are 1841, 1851, 1861, 1871, 1881 and 1891. The 1901 returns will be open to the public in 2002 and the 1911 returns in 2012.

Last time new returns became available, a long queue of anxious and excited researchers formed outside the Census Office overnight in order to be first to obtain the information they were seeking. Whereas genealogists and family historians were once the only people interested in the Census Returns, historians and sociologists have now become aware of the value of the Census and frequently use them as a basis for research into Victorian society and as a comparison to support their theories and researches relating to the present day.

The Census Office is part of the Public Record Office and the new census rooms were opened in July 1990 in the basement of the Public Record Office in Chancery Lane. The Census Office issues a small but very informative seven page leaflet (with two maps attached) Number 58, entitled 'How to use the Census Rooms'. Send a self-addressed foolscap-size envelope to the Public Record Office, Chancery Lane, London, WC2A 1LR, requesting a leaflet before your visit.

To find the census rooms, enter the Public Record Office by the main entrance in Chancery Lane and follow the very clear signposts along the corridors and down the stairs to the census rooms. Security is very strict at the PRO and you will be asked to show the contents of any bags you may have with you.

At the bottom of the stairs is a small desk where a security officer will ask you to sign a visitors' book, giving your name and address; you will be given a plastic pass on a chain with a number on it which you will also enter against your name in the visitors' book. A quick glance through the page offered for your signature will reveal that researchers at the census rooms come from all over the world. No other requirements are made of searchers, no readers' permits are required and no fees are charged. As with all archives, opening times may alter and it is always safer to telephone to check for any changes before setting out on a wasted journey. The plastic pass will give you the number of the microfilm machine which is allocated for your use. Most searchers put the chain over their heads and wear the plastic card like a necklace, leaving hands free for work.

At the end of a long corridor is the entrance to the census rooms. Near the security desk is a cloakroom where you must leave any coats or bags – you are allowed to take only one small bag, notebooks and pencils into the census rooms. Only pencils may be used, so do not forget to take your "travel pack". Pencil sharpeners are, however, provided.

The first room on the left of the corridor is a "rest room". There are chairs and low tables and a drinks vending machine. Here you may relax if you need a break and eat any food you have brought with you. If you intend spending a day in the census rooms (and you will probably spend many once you start your research) take a packed lunch with you to make the best use of your time. I have to admit that I find searching the census returns a rewarding and fascinating part of family history research. Food and drink may not be consumed in the research rooms but time spent in the rest room will not be wasted since you may well learn more from other searchers to assist your research. Family historians are always willing to share their experiences and knowledge when they have the time.

The original records are not available to the public but can be seen on microfilm; your plastic card will give you the number of your machine. There are seven rooms of machines; at the entrance to each the numbers of the machines in that room are shown. There are over 200 machines available, provided on desks in rows, each with its own seat and they are quite simple to use. There is not much space between the machines, but there is sufficient room on the desk beside your machine for your notebook.

The film, which comes in a box, is on a reel which fits onto the spindle at the front on the left of the machine, runs under a frame and is threaded up onto an empty film reel on another spindle on the right. A handle on each spindle enables you to wind the film backwards and forwards and to stop at any point. There are two switches on the machine, one to turn it on and a light switch. The picture on the film is thrown up onto a screen on the machine and can be regulated and brought into focus by turning a small wheel. If you watch the person using the machine next to you for a few minutes you should find it fairly easy. The information leaflet Number 58 gives clear illustrated instructions on how to use the machines.

If you have put the film in backwards, do not be deterred, just take it off and turn it round. Handle the film carefully, try not to put your finger marks on it and try not to drop it. If you do, you will have the trouble of rewinding it by hand since the film, if dropped, tends to unwind itself very quickly despite all your efforts to catch it.

Using a microfilm machine requires concentration and can be quite tiring for the eyes and the back of the neck because of the angle when looking at the screen, particularly if you are either taller or shorter than average. In addition, some of the films are difficult to read since they are films of hand-written documents. The writing can be difficult to decipher in some cases and the film makers were not always careful. Films can be too light or too dark. A short rest away from the machine at regular intervals is refreshing and gives renewed energy.

It is not possible to book a machine in advance so it is advisable to go the census rooms early. In the summer months a queue may form and the security officer will give you an idea of how long you might have to wait for a machine. It is not much use popping into the census rooms if you only have a limited time to spare.

The first room leads into the 'Reference Room'. Here you will find the reference books which will help you find the numbers of the films (the 'piece references'). Census returns are not indexed by names, but by villages, towns, districts and counties. London, the Greater London area and some other large cities are indexed by streets, making the research easier. The basis for your research will be the addresses on the birth, marriage and death certificates you have obtained, those you have been given by members of your family and found during your original research amongst family documents. Those on the certificates will also have a precise date and your research will begin in the census year nearest to that date.

There are separate sets of books, colour coded, for each of the years 1841, 1851, 1861, 1871, 1881 and 1891 and for London. Each year has a main index of place names showing which number book to look in to find the reference number of the film for the place you wish to research. The reference numbers consist of letters and numbers. Clear instructions on how to use these indexes are displayed on the walls in the reference room and are very easy to follow. In addition, there is a desk where attendants will explain how to find the reference numbers.

If you are unable to find a place name in the index books it could be because of changed boundaries or spelling. Ask the attendants for help, explaining what you are looking for – they are very helpful. Sometimes other researchers, if you explain you are a beginner, will give you assistance, but do not presume on their good nature, their time is as valuable as yours.

If you have several addresses to research, look up all the reference numbers while you are in the reference room, which will save you several journeys back to this room. Always make a careful and correct note in your notebook of the 'piece reference'. You may need to return for further research another day and it will save time not to have to look through the indexes again. It will also assist others in your family if they wish to help with the family history research.

When you have made a note of all the film numbers you require, make your way out of the reference room to the microfilm machine reading rooms. As mentioned above, the entrance to each room shows the numbers of the machines in that room.

Films are in cabinets in most reading rooms and are available on a 'help yourself' basis. The cabinets are clearly marked for each year and the drawers are marked showing the 'piece reference' numbers contained in each drawer. At the side of your machine is a black box the same size as the boxes in which the films are kept. This box is your marker and shows the number of your machine. Taking your marker with you, go to the set of drawers which contains the films you require. Take the film you require and put your marker in its place. This helps you to find the place when you return the film and also allows other researchers to know that that particular film is in use. When you find an entry you are looking for, copy it in detail, leaving nothing out. Other occupiers of the premises, visitors or lodgers, may be members of the family, in-laws or cousins with different surnames.

When you have finished with your film, rewind it onto the main spool and return it in its box to the cabinet. At the same time, remove your own marker from the cabinet. You can continue in this way to search all the films you wish to use. When you have finished, return your last film to the cabinet and leave your marker beside the microfilm machine, ready for the next searcher.

If you wish for photocopies of the relevant census returns, these can be obtained from the photocopying room. There are instructions on the wall in that room telling you how to obtain the copies and how much they will cost. Read those instructions before you start your research so that you will have some idea of what to do. The attendants in the photocopying room will deal with your request. Some of the very old returns do not make very satisfactory copies, but the attendants do their best to give you a fair copy.

The 1841 returns are the least informative, giving only the names of the occupants of each house, shop, hospital,

workhouse and all occupied buildings on the night of 7th
June 1841. Ages are not specific except for those under 15
years of age. Over 15 years the ages are rounded up or
down to the nearest 5 years. Divisions between families
are shown and between houses and also occupations, but
relationships in which you are interested are not shown.
There is a column showing "where born" in which initials
are used. "Y" means "Yes, born in county of present
residence", "N" means "No, not born in county of
present residence", but no indication is given of where
actually born. "I" means "born in Ireland", "S" "born in
Scotland" and "F" "born in foreign parts", again giving
no specific place of birth.

The returns for the following years are much more
informative giving detailed information very helpful to the
family historian. The details given in the years 1851
onwards are the names, the head of the house and the
relationships to the head of the house of every other
person present at the time of the Census, whether they
were married, their ages, occupations and exact places of
birth. The 1851 and 1861 returns show those who were
blind, deaf or dumb and the 1871 and 1881 ones also
indicate those who were idiots and lunatics.

Although people were supposed to answer the Census
questions truthfully, they did not always do so. Do not,
therefore, rely entirely upon the information found in
the Census returns, check it against all the other information you have. Ages were often incorrect. If you are able
to follow a female relative through several Census returns,
you may find that she remains the same age over a period
of 30 years or mysteriously grows younger. I had one
relative who in 1851 gave Scotland as his birthplace, in
1861 England and in 1871 decided to give Scotland again.
Such discrepancies can be confusing, but put together with
all the other information you have gathered, will sort itself

out in the end and you should be able to decide which is the fact and which the fiction, but not always. There will always be question marks against some of the names in your family history.

When you have finished your research, gather up your notes and collect your coat and bags from the cloakroom. Return your plastic pass to the security officer at the desk where you first signed in and follow the signs to the exit of the PRO.

Scotland

The Census returns for Scotland can be seen at New Register House, Edinburgh. A search charge is made and it is necessary to book in advance by letter or telephone in order to reserve the microfilm machine. This does, however, eliminate a queue and the films are provided very quickly. The original Census records including 1891 are also available to researchers.

The original Census returns for Scotland had to be sent to England and were then returned to Scotland. Unfortunately, parts of the 1841 Census for the County of Fife were lost at sea on their way home and are not available in any form. If yours were lost, there is no alternative but to give up using the Census for that line of research.

Ireland

Census records in Ireland can be seen at the Public Record Office in Dublin. These records have suffered losses caused, not only by fire, but also by deliberate destruction based on a decision made by the government, as in the case of the 1861 and 1871 records. There are, however, many Census records still available to the family historian and you may well find what you are seeking.

The Isle of Man

The Census records of the Isle of Man are available at Chancery Lane and the Reference Library of the Manx

Museum. A useful piece of information given on these records is the place of birth of the person recorded. If the person was born off the island, the country of birth is given.

The Channel Islands

The Census records for all the Channel Islands are available at the Chancery Lane Census Office on microfilm and can be searched as described above. The Census records for Jersey are also available on microfilm at the Central Library in St. Helier in Jersey.

Why are you at the Census Office and what are you looking for? The Census returns give a great deal of information about where families lived, what they did, and family relationships. This will be the first time during your researches that you will see official records of different branches of your family in groups. Up to now the certificates you have obtained have been either for one person or for two people if a marriage certificate.

When you look at the Census returns for your own family, take time to look at the surrounding houses and buildings, the occupations and names of neighbours, the sizes of the families. All this will begin to give you an idea of the environment in which they lived and the lives they led. In cities many families herded together in single dwelling houses, others occupied large houses with servants. Workhouse inmates are shown as well as hospital patients. Occupations can also give an indication of the area in which people were living. Very often people engaged in the same or ancillary occupations grouped together and lived in one street. Street names were occasionally changed to reflect this. Fathers who had a trade taught their sons. Following through the ten year cycles, sons grow up, take over their fathers' occupations and themselves become "Head of the house" although if a widowed mother is left she will sometimes be given as the

"Head of the house", Apprentices lived with their masters and many city dwellers let rooms to lodgers. In rural areas different branches of the same family lived near to each other and you could find a lead to take you on to another branch of the family.

Between one Census return and another, you may lose someone. Check the information given. They may have moved away or they may have died. If they died, their spouse would be shown as widow or widower. This would give you a clue to the date of death if you do not already know it. It must have been between the dates of the two Census returns. This would pinpoint the date more closely and possibly save much time searching the death records. Look in the adjacent streets for their names. They may have been visiting a neighbour at the time the Census was taken. The other alternatives are hospital, school, or prison. Remember that house numbers, street names and boundaries may have changed between two Censuses. If you have noted the names of neighbours on previous Censuses and they are still in occupation of adjacent houses then your family must have moved away. If all the families have disappeared they may be recorded elsewhere under a different street name.

Search each return from 1841 onwards, gradually assembling a picture of the family, its occupations and movements during those years.

Take a look at the marriage certificate of your grandparents or great grandparents (according to your own age the year of their marriage will be earlier or later) which you should have found without too much difficulty by following the instructions given in previous chapters. Once again using my Smith family as an example, we have the marriage of William Charles Smith and Sarah Ann Dean which took place in Dartford in Kent in 1876. The certificate gives the actual place of residence at the time of the marriage of both the bride and the groom. The groom was living at 1 Mount Pleasant Road, Dartford and the bride at Chalk Row, Dartford. Taking the nearest Census date 2 April 1871, we can request the microfilm for each house. Hopefully Sarah Ann Dean and William Charles Smith or at least one of them were living with their parents in their family homes at the time of the marriage. If they were not, their families may be living there or may have only recently moved there. A search of the previous 1861 Census for the same address will give the answer. If it is the family home the Census return will give us the names of their parents and other information, taking us back one generation further and possibly even more.

The Census returns for 1871 show that Sarah Ann Dean was living with her parents at Chalk Row, Dartford. Her father Alfred Dean was the head of the house, his age was 46, sex male, occupation Army, and that he was born in Dartford. Her mother Ann is shown as "wife". Her age is 43, sex female, occupation housewife and place of birth Maidstone. All the children of the family are shown including Sarah Ann – daughter – age 21 unmarried – whose occupation is shown as seamstress. An interesting point is that Sarah Ann and two of her brothers were born in India, probably while their father was in service in the Army – a point well worth following. In addition to the family there is an entry for Alice Brown, a servant, and William Cross, a lodger.

The birth certificate of George William Joseph the son of Sarah Ann and William Charles, dated 1878, shows them living at 81 Mount Pleasant Road, East Hill, Dartford. A search of the 1881 census for that house reveals all the family of Sarah Ann and William Charles, thus filling gaps in your family tree and spreading the branches further.

Sometimes you may be lucky enough to find visiting relatives or in-laws which can carry your research further. Figure 14 is an example of what you might expect to see in the Census returns.

The enumerators used abbreviations to save time and room on the forms when making their entries. Some of the more common abbreviations are:

Ag.Lab. – Agricultural Labourer
App. – Apprentice
Dom. – Domestic servant
H. – Head of household
Lab. – Labourer
N.K. – Not known
Serv. – Servant.

Most abbreviations are easily deciphered but if you have any doubts about the meanings ask one of the attendants.

If you feel that you need a sight of the next two Censuses after the cut-off year to further your research, a request for a search can be made. The Census Office will require an exact address and the name of the person. They will search for only one address and not the surrounding properties. It is essential, therefore, to get the address correct. If your family is living in the house next door, that information will not be given. There is a special form on which to apply for this search and the applicant must be a direct descendant or be acting on their behalf. The applicant must also confirm that any information given will not be used for litigation purposes. The only information the Census Office will supply if the search proves positive is the age and place of birth of the named person or persons.

This form of search is quite expensive and the fee has to be paid in advance. If no entry is found there is no refund. A leaflet giving details of this service is available from the Chancery Lane Office. If you have come to a dead end in your research it may be worth paying the search fee in order to get started again. At this early stage in your work

PARISH OF HACKNEY

Name of Street, Place or Road and Name or No. of House	Name and Surname of each Person who abode in the house, on the Night of the 30th March 1851	Relation to Head of Family	Condition
21 Millfields Road	HENRY DANIEL	Head	Widower
	ELIZA DANIEL	Dau	Unm
	JOHN FOX	Lodger	Unm
	FRANK WILLIAM GREEN	Lodger	Unm
	ELEANOR CROSS	Serv	Mar
23 Millfields Road	SUSAN BERKLEY	Head	Mar
	HENRY HOLCOME	Son	Unm
	ALICE HOLCOMBE	Dau	Unm
	BENJAMIN BERKLEY	Son	Unm
	CHARLES BERKLEY	Son	Unm
25 Millfields Road	THOMAS SMITH	Head	Mar
	MARY SMITH	Wife	Mar
	JOAN BANKS	Niece	Unm

Fig. 14 What you might see in the 1851 census return

Age of male	female	Rank, Profession or Occupation	Where born	Whether Blind or Deaf and Dumb
57		Manager at Bank	Norfolk, Norwich	
	27		Middlesex, London	
24		Bankers Clerk	Surrey, Old Kent Rd.	
40		Porter in a bank	Herts, Watford	
	30	Housekeeper	Kent, Dartford	
	38	Shop manageress	Middlesex, Hackney	
16		Scholar	Middlesex, Hackney	
	14	Scholar	Middlesex, Hackney	
12		Scholar	City of London	
8		Scholar	City of London	
39		Coalman	Middlesex, Tottenham	
	35		Northumberland, Newcastle	
	19		Northumberland, Newcastle	

it should not be necessary to go to that expense as there are so many other avenues to follow if one is blocked.

8
PARISH REGISTERS

When you have exhausted all the research sources offered by civil registration records, where can you look for pre 1837 information? There are many pre-registration sources. The details gained from your Census research and copy certificates can lead you to probably the most important which are the Parish Registers.

Parish Registers, which were handwritten, contain records of baptisms, marriages and burials and were instituted in 1538 by Thomas Cromwell, during the reign of Henry VIII. They relate to the established Church of England. However, all the earliest registers have not been preserved, and you may find that the records of the parish in which you are interested start much later. The information given in each register was at the discretion of the parish clerk and may vary from parish to parish and from year to year in each parish. A diligent and conscientious clerk would give the maximum and a lazy clerk the minimum.

The parish registers were normally in the charge of the vicar or incumbent of each church, but in 1979 a law was enacted to ensure the protection and preservation of parochial records. If a local incumbent was not able to keep the documents in a suitably safe environment the records had to be desposited elsewhere in a record office covering the diocese of that church. The usual place was the County Record Office. The diocesan Record Offices also have the power to request that any parish registers still held by a local incumbent be deposited with them on loan for a period of one year. Under the 1979 Law, County Record Offices may not make an inspection charge for parish registers deposited with them, although they may have a general search fee and a fee for use of microfilm and microfiche machines. Incumbents are allowed to charge a fixed inspection fee. Incumbents are legally bound to allow any registers they hold to be inspected, but they have no duty to search the registers themselves in response to requests by letter. However, many will do so but although they may be willing, they may not be experienced or efficient researchers. They may miss just the point that you are seeking to confirm. If you seek their assistance a donation to the church funds sent with the request would probably be appreciated.

If you wish to inspect a parish register, first enquire from the local Records Office whether they hold that register. If they do not, they will be able to advise the name and address of the incumbent who does hold that register, or any other place where it is held. If you require the name and address of the present incumbent of any parish church, this can be obtained from Crockfords Clerical Directory which should be available in your local reference library. If the register is still held by the incumbent, write (enclosing a stamped addressed envelope for reply) or telephone in advance of your visit, requesting an appointment and listing the registers you wish to inspect. This will help the incumbent and also save time, which may be limited. Make a list for yourself, chronologically, which is the way the registers are kept, and by name. Include the surnames of all the families you are researching, cousins, in-laws and any other relatives so that you can make the most use of your visit. Do not forget the ever important notebook and pencils, magnifying glass and money to pay for copies and fees. Make a very careful and exact copy of the records you find, together with a note of the source and references in case you wish to return for further research. Follow exactly the names, spellings, and dates even if they are different from what you expected to find. Copy all the references to your surname however remote the relationship might seem, they may well fit into your family tree somewhere on a distant branch. In some Record Offices you can obtain photocopies of the pages of the parish registers, which can be added to your supporting documents file.

Bishops' Transcripts

Commencing with the year 1597, a full copy of each parish register had to be sent to the diocesan Bishop each year. Many of the Bishops' Transcripts, referred to by family historians and genealogists as "B.T's", are easier to read than the original parish registers and are available at County Record Offices sometimes on microfilm or microfiche. There are also some B.T's commencing in 1561 but these are not comprehensive. All the B.T's for Wales are held in the National Library of Wales. Bishops' Transcripts are by no means complete records since parish clerks did not always comply with the instructions given. In addition mistakes were made by the parish clerks in transcriptions from the registers, and full returns were not always made. They may be helpful however, if original parish registers have been lost. Many Bishops' Transcripts were lost or destroyed, including those for the diocese of St. Paul's Cathedral, lost in the great fire of London in 1666. B.T's should be used as an aid, and any entries found should be checked with the original parish registers if possible.

The Calendar

It is important to know that before 1751, following the

Julian Calendar, the church year began on Lady Day 25
March and ended the following 24 March. The Gregorian
calendar then came into use giving 1 January as the first
day of the year and 31 December the last. In order to
catch up with the alterations in the calendar, in 1751 25
March became the first day of the year and 31 December
the last, giving 1751 only 9 months. In 1752 the year commenced on 1 January and ended on 31 December, but 14
September followed 2 September leaving out 11 days. In
1753 and from then onwards the year began on 1 January
and ended on 31 December. When recording entries between 1 January and 24 March for the years prior to 1750,
both the old and present day style of dating should be
shown. E.g. 23 February 1731 should be shown as 23 February 1731/1732, the historical date being 1732 but the
church date being 1731 (This applies *only* to the dates
between 1 January and 24 March).

Kings and Queens

Some early documents do not give an exact date, but
refer to a time in the life of the reigning monarch. E.g.
"on the twelfth day of August in the ninth year of the
reign of our Gracious Queen Elizabeth". This requires a
little extra research into the exact date the monarch in
question ascended to the throne. The reign of George IV
commenced on 29 January 1820, making the year 29
January 1820 to 28 January 1821 the first year of his reign,
and 29 January 1822 to 28 January 1823 the 3rd year of
his reign. The practice of dating documents using what are
known as regnal years was not used during the Interregnum
or Commonwealth years 1649 to 1660 and ceased after the
reign of Queen Victoria whose first year as Queen began
on 20 June 1837. After the restoration of the monarchy,
at the end of the Interregnum, the reign of Charles II was
backdated to the death of Charles I and was deemed to

have commenced on 30 January 1649. In the Appendix I give the dates of the commencement of each reign up to and including Queen Victoria.

The Marriage Act 1753

In 1754 an Act promulgated in 1753 by the then Lord Chancellor Lord Hardwicke was enforced. The Act, which covered England and Wales was designed to reduce the number of clandestine marriages. It standardised the performance of marriages and the entries to be made in parish registers. Parents or guardians had to give consent to marriages of minors. Banns had to be called or marriage licences issued before a marriage could take place in a church or chapel, failing which the marriage was not valid. Full and proper details of the marriage had to be entered in the register on printed forms, thus providing more information for the family historian. The Act did not affect those of the Jewish or Quaker religions who were allowed to marry within their own religions provided a proper registry was kept. Roman Catholics were not excluded from the Act. This Act led to clandestine but legal marriages taking place over the border in Scotland where the consent of parents to a minor's marriage was not required. If you are unable to find a marriage record you are seeking in a local parish register, don't forget Gretna Green in Scotland where many marriages took place. A couple might then return to their parish where no record of their marriage existed, but the birth of their first child might show in the parish register, leaving the family historian with a missing piece of the puzzle. Until 1929 boys were allowed to marry with parental consent from the age of 14 years and girls with consent from the age of 12 so do not be surprised at the dates of marriages compared with birth dates. In 1929 the minimum age for marriage for both boys and girls became 16 years. These points should be taken into consideration when searching for marriages.

During the period of the Civil War and the Commonwealth that followed, between 1641 and 1660, bishops were abolished and the keeping of registers was abandoned by many parishes. Licences were not issued and marriages were performed under Civil Law by authorised ministers, J.P.s and magistrates. There is therefore a fairly large hole in the run of parish registers.

It is essential to search all the registers of a parish, commencing with the latest and working back to the earliest. Make a note of all entries relating to surnames connected with your family. Do not assume that you have a complete record from one parish register. Families moved about then as they do now. They could have left the parish before all the children were born, or come to the parish from another bringing some children baptised elsewhere with them.

Baptism

The information in parish registers relates to baptisms – not births. If a child was not baptised there will be no record of the birth in the parish register. There are a number of reasons why a baptism did not take place. The parents could have been non-conformists, Quakers, Jews or Roman Catholics. A baptism could have taken place in a nearby parish if, as was common, a young wife returned to her mother's house for help with the birth of her child. A child born in a city to country born parents may have been taken back to the country parish for baptism. Not all baptisms took place near the time of the birth. Sometimes if a child was born early in a marriage the parents could not afford the baptism fee. As they prospered and the families grew, a whole family could be baptised at the same time after the birth of several children, in which case their respective ages may be given. Some baptisms refer to adults and not children. If you are doubtful, try to check elsewhere. The B.T's might help. Illegitimate children were often baptised and reference made in the register to their illegitimacy with, occasionally, the father also named.

The information given for a baptism will be the date, christian names of the child, parents' christian names with the father's surname (mother's surname for an illegitimate child), where they lived (village or town), profession of father and by whom baptised.

It was not compulsory to give the age at baptism and often that information was omitted, making it difficult for the family historian to find an exact date of birth from parish registers. It was the baptism which was important at that time, not the age of the person being baptised. It may be necessary to try to find evidence of exact dates elsewhere if possible, from monumental inscriptions, family bibles, other family documentation or entries in the parish registers relating to other members of the family. Dates and ages were not so important in parish registers which were meant to be records of religious events.

Marriages

Marriages are more likely to be shown in parish registers than are baptisms, since most were performed by the church, although not always in the expected parish. From 1754 onwards the banns had to be called or licences issued. Banns had to be called in the parish of the proposed bride and groom and the marriage could have taken place in either parish. It was only necessary to have been a resident in a parish for three weeks to enable a marriage to take place. One or other of the couple could come from a distant parish or a travelling couple could have decided to remain in a parish for the purpose of marriage and then moved on again. If you are unable to find the entry in the groom's parish, look for it in the bride's parish where the marriage was more likely to have taken place. Banns were usually entered in a separate banns book, but could be entered in the marriage register separately from the marriages. If a marriage was by Licence (which gave permission to marry without the calling of the banns) the fact would be recorded in the register. An application for a Licence would have been for a Licence bond or Allegation and either made to a Bishop or an Archbishop's office. If a register entry shows a marriage by Licence, search for the Bond or Allegation which will give further genealogical information. If there is one, obtain a photocopy for your documents file. Marriages by Licence became quite the fashion in all walks of life, although the licences themselves no longer exist since they were given to the bride and groom when issued and have been lost through the ages.

A marriage entry in a parish register will give the names of both parties, the occupation of the groom, the names of their respective parishes, and their status, (spinster, widow, bachelor, widower). If the bride is shown as a widow, remember that her surname will be that of her former husband and not the family surname, leaving you with further research. If either or both of the parties to the marriage were minors and the marriage by consent of parents or guardians that fact will be shown. This would show that the consenting parent was alive at the time of the marriage, another piece of useful information. The names of two and sometimes three witnesses are also given in the register. These are of particular interest as they could be other members of the family. If the same name as a witness appears at other marriages in the register this may have been a professional witness or the parish clerk. It is worth checking the surrounding marriages if only to eliminate that name from your researches.

Burials

The information in parish registers relates to burials –

not deaths, although burials usually took place within a few days of the death. Once again the deaths of non-conformists, Quakers, Jews and Roman Catholics will not be entered. The information given in relation to a burial is often only the name and age of the deceased and the date of burial. Other information shown might in the case of a female be "widow or wife of - - - - -" and in the case of children "son or daughter of - - - - -".

Parish Register Copies

Many parish registers have been copied, with some copies available in printed form. The printed copies can be seen in County Record offices, libraries and the Society of Genealogists in London. Local family history societies sometimes hold copies relating to the parishes in their own areas. These should only be used as an aid since as with all transcriptions they do contain errors and omissions but they are helpful as a guide where to look and what records exist. Also held at the Society of Genealogists is "Boyd's Marriage Index" which in a series of volumes indexes marriages in several counties from 1538 to 1837. Copies of this index on microfilm can be seen in some County Record Offices, and reference libraries.

Parish registers can, like the Census returns, reveal the way of life followed by our ancestors. How large families were, how they moved about, how long people lived. A sudden increase in burials one year could indicate an illness sweeping through a parish or a bad winter. There is much more to be learned from parish registers than names, dates and places.

Other Registers

If your ancestors were followers of a religion other than that of the established Church of England, they were known as non-conformists or dissenters and were excluded from many laws, such as Hardwicke's Marriage Act of 1753.

Roman Catholic

Registers of births and marriages were kept by Roman Catholic churches and some still remain in the possession of the priest in charge of local churches. Some registers are held in the Public Records Office or have been deposited in local County Record Offices. Roman Catholics were frequently buried in local parish churchyards and their burials were recorded in the general parish registers. If you wish to trace an ancestor of the Roman Catholic religion, contact the archivist of the Roman Catholic diocese concerned. He will know the present whereabouts of the parish registers. Alternatively, The Catholic Family History Society (see Appendix) may be able to help you with your research.

Jews

Jews lived in many parts of England, but the largest community was in London. Most synagogues kept records of their congregations. Some Jews paid for their children to be included in local parish registers. If such entries were made they stated "son or daughter of a Jew". There are many such entries in parish registers of City of London churches. Marriages were not always recorded, but brides had to be given a marriage contract and often deposited copies with the synagogue. Burials were recorded in the records of Jewish burial grounds. For information of the records available, write to the synagogue in the area in which you are interested, asking what documentation is available. There is also a Jewish Museum in London where original records can be seen.

Quakers – The Society of Friends

Of all the non-conformists, the Quakers kept the most extensive and informative records. Some have been deposited at County Record Offices and some at the Public Record Office. Before being deposited, many of the original records were transcribed and are held by the Society of Friends. The records have been indexed and upon payment of a fee can be seen at the Library of the Society of Friends in London.

Protestant Non-Conformists

Baptists, Methodists, Presbyterians, United Reform Church and Congregationalists, all kept records of the births, marriages and deaths of their congregations. Here again some records have been deposited with local County Record offices and some with the Public Record Office. Many remain with the local congregations. Write to the local chapel or church asking for information as to the whereabouts of the documents you are seeking. There is a Baptist Historical Society in London, a Methodist Archive Collection in Manchester, and a Presbyterian Historical Society in London.

Huguenots

Huguenots were French, but many also came to England from Holland or Germany. They settled mainly in London, Bristol, Canterbury, Colchester, Norwich, Plymouth, Rye, Sandwich and Southampton. Their records have been deposited in local County Record Offices and the Public Record Office. If there was no local French church, baptisms were carried out by the local parish church and the records appear in parish registers. Deaths generally are not documented except for those that occurred at the London Huguenot Hospital. Check with the local archives to see what is available or contact the Huguenot Library in London.

Scotland

The Parish registers in Scotland can be seen on microfilm at New Register House in Edinburgh. A search fee is charged and it is necessary to make an appointment as in the case of searching the civil registration records. However, since all the records are under one roof, one day may cover a great deal of research.

Not many parish registers survive before 1700. There are more registers for Glasgow and Edinburgh than for country areas. The information given for baptisms often includes the maiden name of the mother which is helpful. Some registers have been indexed and transcribed. The Society of Genealogists in London holds copies of some areas of Scotland on microfilm.

Parish Registers in Ireland

Many parish registers in Ireland were deposited in the Irish Record Office in Dublin and were destroyed by fire in 1922. Do not be put off by this generalisation concerning Irish records. Many records were transcribed and copied locally before they were sent to Dublin and some were not sent to Dublin at all. Copies of most of the parish registers are available in Dublin at the National Library. There are registers for both Catholic and Protestant churches. The Catholic registers are usually written in Latin and some help may be required in translation.

Original registers are usually held by local parish priests and parish clerks and the usual written approach can be made. Try the local parish priest by writing, setting out clearly the information you are seeking. You cannot expect a busy parish priest to do your research for you, or he may not have the expertise, but a polite request accompanied by a contribution to the upkeep of the church may bring a very helpful response. There are many parish registers on microfilm and some local Family History Societies have detailed information concerning their parish registers.

While on the subject of Ireland, if you have any form of enquiry and you know the parish concerned, it is always a good idea to write to the present parish priest. He is usually very knowledgeable about his own area and its history or can point you in the right direction. A written request accompanied by a reply paid envelope and a donation to church funds often produces a great deal of information concerning the history of a family.

Isle of Man

Copies of parish registers on microfilm or microfiche can be seen at the reference library of the Manx Museum. Original parish registers are held in various places, but an enquiry made to the local church or the Museum will enable you to find out where they were held and what is available. The usual stamped addressed envelope is not of much help since the Isle of Man have their own postage stamps. A postal order to cover the cost of postage or an International Reply Paid Coupon can be used.

The Channel Islands

Parish registers in the Channel Islands are mostly still held by the incumbents of the local churches in Jersey, Guernsey and the other islands. Write first to the present incumbent to ask which records they now hold or whether they know where the records you are seeking are held. The usual stamped addressed envelope is not of much help since the Channel Islands have their own postage stamps. An International Reply Paid Coupon available from your own Post Office should be used.

If you are directed by your searches to other religions, always write to the local church, chapel or meeting house (with the usual stamped addressed envelope for reply) stating that you are compiling a family history and what records you are seeking. If they do not hold the records themselves they will almost certainly know where they have been deposited or be able to direct you where else to apply.

9

WILLS, PROBATE AND MONUMENTAL INSCRIPTIONS

Wills provide a very important source of information for the family historian since they often contain references to several members of the family, even when they are excluded, giving their full names and relationships to the deceased person, known as the testator (male) or testatrix (female). The name and address of the person asked to administer the will, executor (male) or executrix (female) would also be given. If a beneficiary was a distant relative or one who had moved away, the address might also be given. A will could also introduce you to a previously unknown member of the family or show a connection with a distant branch. If there was no will, but property (the estate) was left, a member of the family or several of them together could apply to be executors by means of Letters of Administration which took the place of a will. In this case the full names and addresses of the proposed executors together with their relationship to the deceased would be given. A will could also give guidance as to the place of burial where a tombstone or monument might give the names of other members of the family and family relationships.

Many people, even the poorest, made wills, some of them being "deathbed wills" dictated to a close friend or church representative just prior to death. Women bequeathed their "best bonnet with the blue ribbons", "my large copper pan" or "my second best grey woollen skirt". Men bequeathed "my milking cow with calf", "one shilling" or "my heavy working coat". Blankets and feather beds were frequently bequeathed as were single items of furniture such as chairs, dressers and beds. It may seem an odd thing to say, but wills can bring your ancestors to life in many ways. The value of the goods bequeathed can indicate how highly the testator thought of the recipient. Lists or inventories of possessions indicate the wealth of the family and sometimes its standing in the community. I recently assisted a local archive to sort and catalogue a bundle of early handwritten wills, most of which had not been inspected before. The time spent on this work was most rewarding, bringing to light the environment in which people were living. One will was made by a widow who had been a shopkeeper and the inventory attached gave the total contents of the shop, which was a general store, together with all the prices. As I read the will, I could see her in my mind's eye weighing bags of flour and oats, measuring off yards of blue sprigged muslin and lavender silk and dispensing molasses and rum. Another will gave minute details of all the dresses bequeathed by an obvious lady of fashion to her daughters and friends.

Family quarrels can be referred to. Members of the family can be included or excluded by name giving their relationship to the testator. Next of kin could contest a will if they had been excluded, thereby delaying the execution of the bequests. It became the custom to leave a small amount, usually six pence to a disliked relative so that they could not object, giving rise to the saying "cut off with a sixpence".

Before 1882, when a woman married, her possessions and property became the possessions and property of her husband and at her death she had no right to bequeath any of her belongings. Therefore before that date not many women made wills, unless they were widows. In 1882 a law was passed giving married women rights over their own possessions and from that date you may find wills by both male and female members of your family.

Figure 15 is a copy of a will of William Catlett of Sittingborne, one of my husband's ancestors, proved in the Prerogative Court of Canterbury in 1647. It was written

Fig. 15. Copy Will of William Catlett.

Copy Will of William Catlett, 1646

William Catlett of Sittingborne co. Kent gentleman dated 15 March 1646.
To poor of Sittingborne £5.00, of Milton £5.00, of Fong 40/–, of Bapchild 40/–, of Podmersham 40/–.
To Edward Gurland of Sittingborne clerk £5.00. To Mr. Lane of Bridgar clerk £5.00. To Mr. Picard clerk of Bapchild 40/–. To my niece Dickerson of Faversham widow £20.00. To my niece Sampson £20.00. To my cousin John Bix of Bapchild Esq £10.00 and to William his son and to Katherine his daughter £10.00 a piece. To my cousin Nicholas Ady £20. To my cousin Elizabeth Adye alias Smith, sister to said Nicholas £40.00. To my cousin George Hicks £10.00. To my cousin Adye Hicks £10.00. To my cousin Elizabeth Frinde £10.00. To my cousin Ann Bradley alias Brockwell £20.00. To my cousin Elizabeth Bradley alias Upton £10.00. To my cousin William Bradley £20.00. To my cousin William Allen of Morston £10.00. To my cousin Allen of Sittingborne, tailor, £5.00. To my cousin Edward Tomlyn of

Sittingborne £10.00 To my cousin Thomas Currall of Rochester, boatswain £20.00. To Robert Currall and Thomas Currall sons of said Thomas £10 a piece. To Elizabeth Currall daughter of said Thomas Currall £20.00. To John Pawson of Sittingborne £30.00. To my servant Elizabeth Midler £20.00. To Henry Lawrence £10.00. To Solomon Bowell £10.00. To my cousin William Catlett of Fong £20. To my cousin Richard Catlett, son of said William £20.00. To my cousin Susan Allen alias Lambert £10.00. To John Lambert of Blackwale, husband of said Susan 40/–. To my cousin George Catlett of Blackwale £20.00. To John Clench of Starfield £5.00. To Jane Burges alias Sharpe £5.00.

Nuncipat Codicil made about 12 o'clock at night after Tuesday 19 October 1647.

Being put to mind by Samuel Packer on that very night attended on him of some about him that had done him service and that he did not or had not remembered them they would condemn him. Testator said he had done so and given something to poor but not much. Asked who should be executor he answered his cousin John Bix of Bapchild Esq.

Witness. Samuel Packer and John Pawson both of Sittingborne.

Probatum 23 October 1647 by said witnesses and John Bix executor.

by him in 1646 and a death bed codicil was added in 1647. William obviously tried to remember everyone he could think of and mentions no less than thirty four people by name as well as the poor of five different parishes. This will gives many relationships and some parishes where people lived. It is also of assistance in tracing family members since it clearly identifies married women by their maiden and married surnames. The occupations of some beneficiaries are also given. As you will see, this will provides many hours of research if all the names and relationships are to be followed and checked in parish registers. Even those mentioned without giving the relationships have to be checked in case they are family members or for the purposes of elimination if they are not.

It is, of course, necessary to know the date or approximate date and place of death in order to start looking for a will. For pre-registration dates, parish registers may give this information. From the date of compulsory registration, with diligent searching the date of death can be found in the death indexes in St. Catherine's House. Census records can also give a clue. If an elderly person in the family "disappears" in the ten years between one Census return and the next while all the other members of the family can be found, a reasonable assumption is that they have died. This is not always the case, but you could narrow your first search to that period of ten years. Newspaper announcements can also give information relating to deaths and burials. Personal colums sometimes carry entries of anniversaries of deaths paid for by a surviving spouse or son or daughter whose names and relationships are also given.

Pre-Registration Wills before 1858
Many wills were never proved or lodged for registration anywhere, either because it was not necessary to do so,

or the estate was not large enough to warrant the expense. Even when registration became compulsory there was and still is no requirement to prove or register a will or letters of administration with a value below a certain amount. Where there were family disputes there might be several years' delay between the date of death and the proving of a will or letters of administration. Original early wills can be found in many places. Before January 1858 when wills and letters of administration came under the jurisdiction of the Principal Probate Registry, wills could be proved in ecclesiastical or church courts, the main courts being the Prerogative Court of Canterbury (P.C.C.) and the Prerogative Court of York (P.C.Y.). Records of wills for the P.C.C. are held in the Public Records Office and those for the P.C.Y. at the Borthwick Institute in York. It is possible, where a testator left property in more than one parish, that their wills came under the jurisdictions of both courts. Searching for early wills is difficult even if they were proved, since it is necessary to decide in which court the will might have been proved. Start by a process of elimination, searching all the indexes of all the courts known to cover a particular parish where the testator died. If no wills appear in either the P.C.C. or P.C.Y. records, they could appear in the records of the lower courts, many of which are held in local County Record Offices. Bundles of wills deposited by churches and solicitors are also held by County Record Offices and local archives. The Society of Genealogists also hold many documents deposited with them by private persons. Other sources of pre-registration wills are detailed in the leaflet relating to wills and probate available from the Public Records Office. Pre-registration wills for Wales are held in the National Library of Wales, those for Scotland at the Scottish Record Office. Those that survive in Ireland are held in the Public Record Office of Ireland in Dublin.

Principal Probate Registry

Wills from January 1858 onwards are much easier to find. All wills and letters of administration proved in England and Wales are held at the Principal Probate Registry, Somerset House in London. The wills are indexed chronologically with surnames in alphabetical order for each year. Base your search of the index on the date of death obtained from the death certificate, remembering that it could be some years after the date of death that a will or letters of administration are proved. The indexes also give such information as the value of the estate, the address of the testator and the names of the executors. There is no fee charged for a search of the indexes. You can inspect copy wills after paying a fee and submitting an application form – there is a notice in the index room telling you how to apply. You will be able to take notes from the wills (using pencil), and remember to make a careful record of the source of your information, with any references, in case you wish to return for further research. A photocopying service is also available on payment of a fee per page copied, either to be collected personally or mailed to you. You may like to have copies of the original wills, showing your ancestors' signatures, and these can also be ordered, for a fee. Your order form should clearly state that a copy of the original will is required.

Scotland

From 1823 onwards wills for Scotland were proved in the local Sheriffs' Courts where they may still be held. Otherwise, they are all deposited at the Scottish Record Office.

Ireland

Irish wills are once again difficult to trace since many were destroyed in 1922. Indexes, even of those destroyed, do exist and are held in the Public Record Office Dublin. Many wills are also held in the Registry of Deeds in Dublin.

Isle of Man

All the early wills from 1631 are held on microfilm in the Manx Museum. There are also original wills held in the archives which have not yet been indexed. Wills commencing in 1916 are held in the General Registry Office and the originals can be inspected. There is a search fee payable at the Registry.

The Channel Islands

Wills and Probate records for the Channel Islands are held by the Registrar General in Jersey for Jersey and the Registrar General in Guernsey for Guernsey and the other Channel Islands. Postal enquiries in the first instance are recommended.

When searching any indexes for wills it is sensible to take time to search each year for all wills under the family surname which you are currently researching. You may come across a will which looks as though it belongs to you, the address of the deceased or the names of the executors pointing to an association with a known member of your family. You need only request a sight of the originals of those that seem markedly of interest.

When you have found your will or letters of administration, extract as much information as you can to enter in your notebook and transfer to your index cards. Make a note of where the will is kept, the date you saw it and reference number ascribed to the document in case you should need to refer to it again at a later date. Important facts to look for are the following:

1. Name of testator/testatrix.
2. Occupation of the testator.
3. Date of will, date of death and date of grant of probate, which could all be different.

4. Address of the testator when the will was made.
5. Names and addresses of executors and relationship to the testator if given.
6. Names and addresses of all beneficiaries with relationships to testator and to each other (wife, children, brothers, sisters etc).
7. Names of people excluded by definition and relationship to testator.
8. Names, addresses and occupations of the witnesses to the signature of the testator. Witnesses are not allowed to be beneficiaries under a will and possibly will be neighbours, solicitors or their clerks or members of the clergy, not necessarily related to the family. A full note should be taken, if only for the purposes of elimination.
9. Any burial instructions given.
10. Any special bequests, particularly land or houses, that might prove a point of interest for your family history write-up.

If you find some pages of particular interest, such as those with the signatures, names and relationships of beneficiaries or unusual bequests ask for a photocopy for your documents books.

Cemeteries and Monumental Inscriptions

Your researches amongst parish registers, wills and newspapers should enable you to find the burial places of some of your ancestors. Death certificates may also give you a clue. Give yourself the pleasure on a bright summer's day of a visit to a churchyard or cemetery. If the parish registers you are seeking are still held by the local church you could combine the register research with a visit to the churchyard.

Unfortunately inscriptions on old tombstones which can suffer from pollution, vandalism, weathering and general neglect, are fast becoming unreadable. Churchyards are also being cleared and "tidied up". If you find evidence of a burial, make a visit to the churchyard or cemetery a priority amongst your researches before destruction takes place. Take a camera with you. You may be able to obtain pictures of gravestones with monumental inscriptions (usually referred to by family historians and genealogists as M.I.s) for your documents books before they are gone for ever. Many local Family History Societies are recording M.I.s and have recorded some that have now disappeared. Contact your local society to enquire whether they have any records relating to the churchyard in which you are interested. It should be borne in mind that not all burials had tombstones and tombstones were sometimes erected in memory of people who died abroad, particularly members of the forces killed in action. M.I.s can also appear on public war memorials, inside churches on pews which have been dedicated by a family and in stained glass church windows. Local war memorials in particular should not be overlooked since they could give a clue to a missing person whose death you have been unable to establish.

Due to the rapid increase in population, churchyards became overcrowded particularly in cities. By 1820 the overcrowding of churchyards in London reached epidemic proportions and private graveyards or cemeteries began to appear. They were not subject to the same controls as churchyards and their upkeep was generally in the hands of private individuals. Many have since disappeared or been incorporated into public gardens. Local authorities were empowered to establish cemeteries and other cemeteries, such as the famous Highgate Cemetery in London were set up by companies who sold burial plots on a profit-making basis. Some churchyards, local authority cemeteries and the private company cemeteries kept plans, numbering each grave and entering the names of the persons buried. Highgate cemetery which closed in 1975 has records from 1839 showing how burial plots passed from one member of a family to another, the size of the plots and the cost, including descriptions of the memorial stones erected. These records are very helpful if they can be found. Often they will show members of one family buried near to each other with in-laws and connecting families all buried in the same churchyard or cemetery.

The information on a tombstone can be the bare facts such as "John Henry Smith 1820–1888", which is not particularly helpful, but many families purchased plots and several members of one family may be buried together, their tombstone providing names, dates and relationships, added as each person died such as:

John Henry Smith
born in this parish 1820
died of a chill 29 January 1888
beloved husband of Mary Ann
also
Mary Ann Smith
born in the parish of Asprey 1825
daughter of George and Katherine Howes
beloved mother of Henry Smith and Alice Green
who died June 10 1898 aged 73 years
also
Alice Green
daughter of John Henry and Mary Ann Smith
wife of Daniel Green
died April 21 1900 aged 55 years.

An M.I. with this amount of information can be of great help to a family historian, possibly giving details of members of the family not previously identified, or confirming information previously uncertain.

10
THE PUBLIC RECORD OFFICE ·

The Public Record Office (P.R.O.) is a vast repository of records, deeds and documents, one of the finest archives in Europe. The documentation is housed in two separate buildings, one in Chancery Lane in London which holds the medieval and early modern records and one in Ruskin Avenue, Kew, which holds modern departmental records. The Census Returns Office, also at Chancery Lane, about which I have already written in Chapter 7 is the third part of the Public Record Office.

Although many famous documents are on view in the Museum of the P.R.O., such as the Domesday Book, Shakespeare's will and the log book of HMS *Victory*, those most likely to be of interest to you are the ones that record events in the lives of ordinary people, such as divorces, Army, Navy, Air Force and Merchant Seamen records. Additional documentation relates to court cases, government department records including maps and plans, Home, Foreign and War Office, and special groups of people such as Civil Servants, bankrupts, clergymen, criminals, emigrants and many more.

It is necessary to obtain a reader's ticket if you wish to engage in research at the Chancery Lane and Kew departments of the P.R.O., either at the Enquiry Office at Chancery Lane or at the Reception Desk at Kew. Existing but expired tickets can also be renewed at those desks. No charge is made for the reader's ticket which will be issued to you on production of formal proof of your identity such as a driver's licence, passport or bankers card or a letter of recommendation from a suitable professional person (doctor, lawyer, teacher etc.). The same ticket can be used at either branch. The times of opening are shown in the Appendix, but it is always worth a telephone call to ensure that no changes have been made and also to enquire whether the records you wish to see are at Chancery Lane or Kew. The P.R.O. usually closes for two weeks at the beginning of October for stocktaking, making a telephone call at that time of the year most essential.

The rule of using only a pencil applies in all areas of the P.R.O. Readers are requested to take care of any fragile documents entrusted to them and not to put their notebooks on top of the documents nor to trace from them. Readers are allowed to request up to three documents at a time and there is no limit set on the time you may keep the documents. A request in advance for documents to be available on a certain day can be made by telephone the day before or by written request. This is particularly helpful if you know what documents you will require as it saves waiting time, which can be up to thirty minutes. A photocopying service is available at all branches of the P.R.O. and a leaflet giving their fees and charges is available at the enquiry desks.

Kew

Allow a whole day for your visit to the Kew department of the P.R.O., which is a short distance from both the Underground and British Rail stations, has ample parking space and is also served by several bus routes. In most cases you will find your one day will extend to many others. The main reading room is on the first floor with a smaller room for maps and large documents on the second floor. The Enquiry Desk, your first port of call is in the Reference Room which also houses indexes, lists and reference books. There is a self service restaurant and drink vending

machines on the premises of the P.R.O. No food or drink
may be consumed in the reading rooms.

Documents at Kew are ordered by computer in the
Reference Room and it is necessary to have a seat number.
When you have obtained your reader's ticket apply in the
Search Room for a bleeper which will also give you a seat
number. Search the indexes for the reference numbers of
the documents you require and enter the documents and
reference numbers together with your seat number on one
of the computer terminals. If you have never met a computer before or feel a little bewildered, seek assistance
from an attendant. You will soon find out how things work
once they are explained to you, and if you make notes,
you can practise on your own. Remember you can request
up to three documents at a time. When your documents
are ready for collection from the desk, your bleeper will
bleep.

Chancery Lane

The Chancery Lane branch of the P.R.O. has two reading rooms on the ground floor. There is a reference room
on the first floor together with the Probate reading room
and the reading room for large documents and maps. The
reading rooms are known as either the Round Room or
the Long Room. It is not necessary to obtain a seat number
at Chancery Lane. The ordering of documents is again by
computer, but instead of a seat number you quote "Round"
or "Long" according to which room you use for your
research. Hopefully by the time you get to the desk in the
room you have chosen, the documents will be ready for
you. If not, use your waiting time to investigate the books
on the open shelves. There are drink vending machines
but no restaurant; however readers may eat their own food
in the public waiting room. Chancery Lane is in an area
surrounded by the law courts, newspaper offices and com-
mercial offices. There are many self service restaurants,

expensive executive restaurants, sandwich bars and "pub lunches" available.

The P.R.O. publish many leaflets giving details of the records they hold, including a general Information Leaflet and their staff are helpful. They will advise what records are available, how the coded reference system works and how to obtain documents for research. They cannot however, assist with personal research. It is not possible in this book to give an indication of all the records available. There is a published guide available in several volumes from HMSO (Her Majesty's Stationery Office). It is possible that your local reference library or County Record Office will keep copies of this Guide. The following are some of the records available at the P.R.O. which may be of most interest to the family historian.

Divorces

Up to date Divorce records, like Census returns are not available to the public. A rule exists restricting the availability of files for 75 years from the date of the divorce. The indexes nevertheless are available for inspection. Application to see recent papers can be made to the Family Division of the Registry in some cases. Divorce records open for research date from 1858.

Soldiers, Sailors and Airmen

Almost everyone has somebody in the family who became a member of the armed forces, whether a Cavalier or Roundhead in the civil war of 1642–1649, a regular soldier serving in the South African war or Royal Marine serving in the Second World War.

The War Office records held in the P.R.O. are by no means complete, but they are extensive. There was no regular army in England before the civil war. Earls, Barons and Kings raised armies as their needs dictated and no formal records were kept. Any records that were kept were in the hands of the regiments raised which were usually named after their colonels. There are some records relating to the armies of the civil war with regiments listed together with their officers.

More and better service records were maintained after 1660 and many are available for research at the P.R.O., Kew, both for officers and other ranks. Applications for pensions by army widows may give full names, addresses, dates of birth and marriage and names of children. Birthplaces of soldiers can also be found in Casualty Returns, Description Books and Pension Lists. Details of marriages and children are to be seen in Muster Rolls, Discharge Certificates and Regimental Pay Lists. If you are looking for an ancestor who served in any regiment, search the indexes of available material, or tell an attendant what you are looking for. They will be able to direct you to the correct documents.

The Admiralty and Navy Board records are equally detailed and extensive. They relate to Commissioned Officers, Warrant Officers, Ratings and Coastguards, covering all aspects of their service. Various documents giving names, places of birth, ages, and family details are available, such as Continuous Service Engagement Books for the years 1853–1872, Ships' Pay Books, Bounty Papers and Records of Officers' Services. Here again the P.R.O. staff will be able to advise you of the reference numbers and where to look if you are able to give them some information such as dates, or names of ships.

In addition to naval records there are separate records for the Royal Marines covering service records of officers and other ranks. There are records of the Marine Pay Office, Letter and Description Books, all giving details of interest to the family historian.

Air Ministry records relating to personnel are not so

extensive, relating mostly to operational records which do sometimes refer to specific men and women in the service. There is some information available about R.A.F. prisoners of war and casualties.

Wills and Probate

Such records as exist relating to Wills and Probate prior to 1858 are held at the P.R.O., Chancery Lane. Few wills are available but information can be seen in the records of the Probate Courts where wills were proved by the executors in order that they could legally act in accordance with the instructions given in the will. Most wills prior to 1858 were dealt with by ecclesiastical or church courts, mainly the Prerogative Court of Canterbury (P.C.C.) or the Prerogative Court of York (P.C.Y.). Where each will was dealt with depended upon the place of death and the size of the estate of the deceased. After 1769 a Legacy Duty became payable on a grant of probate and the Legacy Duty Registers are held in the P.R.O. These Registers which are unfortunately closed to the public for 125 years from the date the duty was entered in the Register state in which court the probate was granted. There are also records of litigation relating to wills and inventories of goods listed in wills. A preliminary search of the indexes relating to Wills and Probate will give some idea of the material available.

Emigrants and Immigrants

There is no complete index of the names of foreigners entering England for the purpose of immigration, but there are many records in the P.R.O. There are documents relating to alien clergymen, strangers in London, and documents from German, Swiss, French and Dutch churches. There are also Treasury records, Certificates of Aliens, Lists of Immigrants made by Ships' Masters, and Registers of Passenger Lists.

Those leaving England to emigrate are also well represented in the records of the Colonial Office, the Home Office, the Board of Trade and the Treasury. There are lists of criminals deported to America, army pensioners who emigrated to Australia and New Zealand. If your researches lead you to think that one of your ancestors emigrated, it may take you a long time, but you could find him or her somewhere in the records at the P.R.O.

Unclaimed Money

You may have heard stories from your relatives of money due to the family but lost because of lack of evidence, or because "Uncle George married again and we never found out what happened to the money". The stories are various and inventive. There is a department of the Chancery Court that since 1876 has dealt with money deposited by solicitors who were unable to trace the next of kin or beneficiaries of an estate. If you can provide evidence of beneficial interest, the details of such accounts can be inspected free of charge. There are also lists published by the London Gazette which can be seen at the P.R.O. It may be worth a try if you think your family story is founded on facts which you have substantiated by your researches.

The Police

Certain documentation relating to the Metropolitan Police is available at the P.R.O., such as certificates of service from 1889–1900 and registers giving names of those who joined the police and those who left between 1829–1947. If you have a family tradition of fathers and sons joining the police force, you may be able to trace several generations using these records.

There are many other categories of records in the P.R.O. available to you, to help you trace your ancestors, including

Change of Name deeds, Shipping records, Private Con-
veyances or sales of land, Manorial Court Rolls and maps,
Apprenticeship Records, Railway Companies before
nationalisation to name but a few. They are all there
waiting for you. All you need is time, patience and
perseverance.

Pay a short visit to the branch of the P.R.O. which is
nearest to you to collect as much literature as is available
giving details of all the records and familiarise yourself
with the layout of the building. At the same time you can
obtain a reader's ticket and possibly spend a little time
finding out how to use the computer ordering system.
When you have sifted through information in the leaflets,
make a list of any of the records that you think might assist
you and then spend a full day, using all your time there to
best advantage by preparing thoroughly for your visit
before you go.

The P.R.O. are slowly moving all their documents to
the Kew respository which is being enlarged. They do give
notice where possible, but some of the documents you
require may not be available while in transit. During the
time of transition it is always wise to telephone in advance
of a proposed visit to check that the documents you
require are available.

11
MORE SOURCES FOR RESEARCH

Now that you are beginning to build a picture of your family history where else can you look to help you? There are many other sources of information available to you to assist in your search for your living relatives and your ancestors. Even the most experienced family historian or genealogist can get lost and does not always know where to look. Always be ready to listen and take advice. Family historians can be helpful to each other. When you do find a new source, keep a note of the address and telephone number in your Information Book with an indication of what records are available, the times of opening and any fees charged. Make a note of the name of someone who has been particularly helpful. Keep your Information Book up to date when you learn of any changes. You may be able to help someone else with that information.

Telephone Directories

Have you tried telephone directories? You have probably at some time seen your surname in telephone directories and wondered whether there is any relationship to yourself. If you have an uncommon name, once again you are lucky, there will not be so many to choose from. When you have found some addresses from the certificates you have obtained, look through the telephone directories of those areas. Your local library may have a collection of telephone directories in its reference department, either for the present day relating to other areas or old directories relating to your own area. If they do not, they may be able to tell you where you can see them. A telephone call to your local telephone sales department or public relations department might give you the answer.

You may be surprised to find that someone with the same family name is still living at the address given in your certificates. If they are, try phoning them, they can only say no, but they may say yes and another door will open. It would have to be quite a coincidence if they were not a branch of the same family. Alternatively, write to people with the same surname telling them you are working on your family history. Give them a few details of your family and ask if they are a branch of your family. Send a stamped addressed envelope for their reply. Be careful in your approach by letter and telephone. Make sure that you establish a definite relationship, by discussing other relatives before you make any form of personal contact.

Information Available on Computers

A great deal of information is available on computers, particularly on the system of CD-ROM (Compact Disk – Read Only Memory). CD-ROM drives are available to add to your own home computers. The I.G.I. (see page 128) is being updated onto CD-ROM and many libraries and information centres are putting their available information onto CD-ROM. A CD-ROM disk can carry a great deal more information than a floppy disk or a microfilm. The I.G.I. is being up-dated using this new system and now covers 80,000,000 names.

In addition, if you have access to Compuserv on Internet there is a Genealogical Forum where a vast amount of worldwide family history information is exchanged. There may be someone in the Forum who is researching your family name with whom you can exchange information. If you need to know where to find books or research sources it is all there on the Genealogical Forum, for the cost of a phone call.

Television and Radio Programmes

Watch out for factual television and radio programmes, particularly those in your local region, relating in detail historical incidents or events concerning the lives of famous people and places. There have been very interesting and informative programmes about the building of railways, war episodes, village life, church buildings, financial institutions, famous hospitals, children in Victorian times, statesmen, soldiers, and many other subjects. These programmes are often well researched and factually correct. They may throw some light on a subject of interest to you as a family historian, giving you some ideas for sources of research that you had not previously considered. Those about places directly of interest to your family can be very helpful, even if they relate to today. Interviews with local characters on regional programmes can provide odd items of interest, opening up more areas for research.

Early black and white films especially those made in England can show places and buildings long demolished but about which somewhere there must be some written information.

Directories

Street and trade directories can give invaluable assistance in tracing members of your family. These can also be found in local reference libraries and County Record Offices. If you are searching to establish an address in the City of London or a London Borough, the Guildhall Reference Library in the City of London has an extensive collection of street and trade directories commencing as early as the middle of the 18th century. Their collection also extends beyond the London area, covering many parts of the country. The Guildhall have much to offer the family history researcher and genealogist which I will refer to specifically in a later chapter. Most areas, rural and urban, published directories, and families, particularly those in business or tradespeople can be traced through many years in those directories. Directories are also useful if you wish to trace roads or streets. If you find a reference to a family name at a given address in an early directory, you can check that address in the Census returns. If your family appears, you will once again have a grouping and not just one person. Approaching the problem the other way, if a Census return has given the occupation of a member of the family, there may be a trade directory relating to their trade or occupation where their name appears with details of what they did. Anyone connected with a bank or merchant house would probably appear in the Bankers Almanac, another kind of trade directory. Well known directories covering a wider area are Kelly's, Whites and the Post Office directories. Some commence as early as 1750 and continue through to the 1950's. Local directories often give a short history of the surrounding area, mentioning places of special interest, churches, schools, inns, public houses, institutions, working men's clubs, hospitals and workhouses. People mentioned by name will be local gentry, publicans, schoolmasters, town officials and clergymen. Trade and street directories are a rich source of information.

Newspapers and Magazines

Newspaper, periodical and magazine archives are another area for research which should not be overlooked, containing, as they do, news and stories relating to family life. Newspapers were first published early in the 17th century and offer much to the family historian in the way of historical happenings, including names of people and places and pictures. Even the advertisements can tell you something. There are many collections of newspapers both local and national. Some are held on microfilm, others hold the original newspapers bound into volumes. Ask at your local library where you can see newspaper archives.

Try your local newspaper, if you have one. They will probably have copies of their own publications. Early newspapers may be available at your local reference library or County Record Office. The Guildhall in the City of London have a complete collection of *The Times* newspaper on microfilm. They also have copies of the London Gazette. As well as local Record Offices and libraries there is a vast library of national, provincial and overseas newspapers and periodicals held in the British Museum Newspaper Library in Colindale, London. The British Museum Library in Great Russell Street, London also has a collection of newspapers as does the Bodleian Library in Oxford. Reader's tickets should be obtained for both the British Museum Library and the Bodleian Library.

How can newspapers help you? Announcements of births, marriages, divorces and deaths appear in the personal columns. If you have a birth or death certificate search the personal columns near the dates. A birth will give the names of the parents and possibly an address. A death notice often gives the names of several members of the family together with information concerning the burial which might lead you to the churchyard and a memorial stone. A death notice may give an indication of an inquest which could be followed up. Engagement and marriage announcements can also be informative, giving the names of the parents of the intended bride and groom. If one of the parents is a widow or widower the marriage announcement usually gives that information. Photographs of weddings often appear in local newspapers accompanied by descriptions of the occasion, giving names of those present at the reception. On their deaths obituaries of local gentry and other prominent people appear. Details of fatal accidents appear which might finally dispel the family story of how "great uncle George died". Details of Court cases are given and reports of many local happenings which may have affected members of your family. Strikes, house fires,

floods, murders, all are chronicled somewhere in newspapers. Look through the notes you have made from the
information given to you by members of your family. If
there is a particular item of interest with a "near enough"
date, look for it in the newspapers around that date. You
may find full details and a photograph. Not all the stories
you read in the newspapers will be completely factual, but
they may be able to confirm in more detail some family
stories that you have already obtained. We have to
remember that they were written for the reader from a
journalistic point of view with the aim of selling as many
copies as possible. Headlines in particular can be very
misleading. In many cases it will be possible to obtain
photocopies of the items you are seeking which you can
add to your supporting documentation. Advertisements
can also be a source of information. Notices of auctions,
houses for sale, giving the name of the vendor, shopkeep-
ers, and tradesmen offering services. From about 1840
shipping companies offered sailings to Australia and
America, giving details of the names of ships, dates of
sailings and the cost. Theatrical productions are also adver-
tised giving the names of the performers. If one of your
forebears was a travelling player you might follow his progress through newspaper advertisements – "Direct from
the Palace Theatre London" or "Next week at Scar-
borough".

If you do not find any reference to your family in early
newspapers, it is still worthwhile looking through them for
the places where they lived. It will help you to form a
general picture of their lives, the clothes they wore, the
houses they lived in, the work they did, their leisure pur-
suits, the illnesses and disasters they suffered as seen
through the contemporary reports.

County Record Offices
Many counties in England and Wales have a Record

Office, created in an effort to preserve and gather together local records and documents. There are also Record Offices in some of the London Boroughs and one in Edinburgh. They house original parish records, wills, court records, civil records, family archives, manorial documents and many other documents relating to local affairs which have been deposited with them. Some counties have several Record Offices, some only one. Each Record Office has its own rules and regulations, days of closing, and hours of opening. Some of the documents may be available on microfilm only. Before making your journey to the Record Office, make a telephone call to enquire whether you need to reserve a microfilm machine or make an appointment and the hours they are open. This will save time for both you and the archivist. In most Record Offices the rules about not eating or drinking while carrying out research on original documents and the use of pencils only for making notes apply. Make a list of what you are looking for. This will also save time and will assist the archivist who will help you by providing the films or documentation you are seeking. If he is told of your particular interest in a simple manner he will know where to look for the documents which will be most useful to you. The staff in the Record Offices have expert knowledge of the documents in their care and are usually very helpful. You may have to wait a little time while those documents are being found but there will be open library shelves with directories, street maps and books of local interest which may offer sources for research while you wait. There may be a limit to the number of documents you can have for your use at one time, so return a document as soon as you have made your notes and finished with it. Photocopies and copy certificates are obtainable on payment of fixed fees. Take enough money with you to cover these charges, particularly small change since you may need it if you are able to make your own photocopies by putting coins in a machine.

The International Genealogical Index

The Genealogical Society of the Church of the Latter Day Saints in Salt Lake City, Utah, USA, are compiling on microfiche an index of worldwide baptisms and marriages, known as the I.G.I. The reason for this dedicated undertaking which by its very nature can never be finished, is that according to Mormon beliefs they can baptise their ancestors into their faith. Whatever their reasons, their work is greatly appreciated by family historians and genealogists. The I.G.I. is a vast area for research, believed to record over 80 million entries and growing all the time. It is based on the computer records held in Utah. The records are taken from pre-civil registration vital records and church records and relate to persons no longer living, the earliest entry being for the year 1538. The microfiche are purchased by many outlets such as Record Offices, The Society of Genealogists, libraries and Family History Societies. The use of microfiche is a method of recording a large amount of data on a small area of film. A microfiche is about the size of a large postcard and is read by inserting the film, flat into a special machine so that the contents are thrown up onto a screen, similar to those on a microfilm machine. The microfiche is moved about, forwards and backwards, to the right or the left in order to bring into focus the names you are seeking. The microfiche machines are very simple to use.

The index is chronological and alphabetical by surname with the first names also given in alphabetical order, county by county and parish by parish within each county for England and Scotland. Wales and Ireland are each shown as a single unit without counties. It is not a complete record of each county, some counties having better coverage than others. On each microfiche is a list of its contents which should be consulted first to check that you have the correct film and to find out whether the parish you require has been recorded. It is also possible to obtain these lists in printed form from a London research agency, the Mormon Church having given permission for the reprint. The series is not published in order of counties as on the microfiche, but in volumes of geographical areas. These listings also have a very good introduction and explanation of how best to use the I.G.I. indexes.

The information given in the I.G.I. in relation to a baptism is the name of the person, the date, the names of the parents and the parish where the baptism took place. Marriages show the names of both parties, which are cross referenced, the date and the parish. Not all the information is gathered from parish records. There is a column headed "Type" which shows which event is recorded or where the information was obtained. Initial letters are used as follows:

A = Adult christening   M = Marriage
B = Birth   N = Census
C = Christening   S = Miscellaneous
D = Death or Burial   W = Will or Probate
F = Birth or christening of first known child

The I.G.I. in total can be seen at the Society of Genealogists in London. The microfiche of the British Isles are available at the P.R.O., Chancery Lane, and the Guildhall Library in London as well as record offices and reference libraries in other parts of England. The I.G.I. for Scotland is available at the National Library of Scotland in Edinburgh, that for Northern Ireland at the Mormon Branch Library in Belfast, and that for Wales at the Mid-Glamorgan County Library at Bridgend. Many local Record Offices hold the I.G.I. for their own counties as do local Family History Societies. If you wish to carry out research, when you have decided where it is available nearest to you, telephone or write in advance in order to reserve the use of a microfiche reading machine. Instruction on how to read, interpret and evaluate the information contained in the I.G.I., both positive and negative, is deserving of a chapter of its own. The I.G.I. contains an immense amount of data. However, it must be emphasised that the I.G.I. is only an aid to your research, it does have many errors and omissions and any information gained must be checked against the original records.

12
LIBRARIES AND RESEARCH CENTRES

Most librarians and archivists are helpful people, willing to devote their time and interest if you approach them in a sensible and friendly manner. Their time is precious and many people seek their assistance. Polite requests for help and an indication that you are willing to wait will usually achieve better results than demands for instant attention. Make your requests as short as possible, but give as much information as you have. They do not usually have time to hear the whole history of one of your ancestors, leading up to a simple question, much as they may wish to. If you know dates or places, write them down and give them to the librarian so that he can take the information with him when looking for documents for you. There are many places where you can carry out your own research once you have obtained a little help and a nudge in the right direction from an expert.

The Society of Genealogists
The Society of Genealogists was founded in London in 1911 and was granted a Coat of Arms in 1986 to mark the 75th anniverary of its foundation. Its members, numbering about 9,000, are professional genealogists, amateur family historians and anyone interested in family history research. Its headquarters were in Harrington Gardens but due to expansion of their ever growing library they moved to Charterhouse Buildings in the City of London, which was once a silk warehouse, making access easier and their prox-

imity to the other major research centres an advantage for
their members. The Society is a non profit making registered charity whose objects are to promote and encourage
the study of genealogy. Anyone interested in genealogy
and family history research can apply to become a member.
Members pay a yearly subscription, those living outside
London or overseas paying less than those living in London. There are also concessions for retired persons, students and married couples. Non members may use the
library facilities of the Society on payment of search fees,
by the hour, half daily or by the day.

The Society issues a quarterly magazine free to its
members, holds meetings and runs classes on many subjects that fall within the realm of genealogy. Introductory
evenings are run for new members, giving an extensive tour
of the library with instruction on how to use the facilities.

The Society of Genealogists claim that its library is
unique in England and that no other library can offer such
extensive research facilities for the family historian.
Almost all the books are on open shelves, giving researchers immediate access so that time is not wasted waiting for books to be brought by attendants. In addition,
borrowing facilities are available to members by mail, upon
payment by the member of the mailing charges. The books
on the shelves are arranged alphabetically by county with
a separate section for countries and relate to all aspects
of family history. There are local history books, poll books,
directories, county records, genealogical periodicals and
magazines. Details of the Monumental Inscriptions that
have been copied and indexed are available filed under
each County, as are books and information relating to
minority religions. Most of the material held relates to the
period before registration (1837) which makes it all the
more useful.

In addition to printed books the Society holds a large
collection of manuscripts and typescripts deposited with

them by private persons, including family histories. These are available in boxes on open shelves, arranged alphabetically by family names and places. The Society holds a large collection of parish register copies, the largest in the country, in printed, typescript and manuscript form, dating from as early as 1538 through to 1812 and some through to 1837. All are listed in the library catalogue. If you are unable to find the one you wish to see, ask the library attendants, since some of the unbound copies are not on the open shelves. Boyd's Marriage Index, a collection of over 500 volumes indexing marriages between 1538 and 1837 is held by the Society. It covers many counties of England (not Wales or Scotland) and some counties have separate indexes for males and females. Boyd's gives information relating to dates and places of marriages indicating the parish register in which more detailed information can be traced.

Indexes of early marriage licences, wills and apprenticeship records are available. These are particularly useful since you can search them while on a visit to the Society and decide whether a visit to other repositories such as the P.R.O. or County Record Offices to inspect the original documents would prove useful.

The I.G.I. on microfiche is available at the Society covering the whole of the British Isles and much of the world. If you wish to search the I.G.I. it is necessary to telephone or write in advance to reserve the use of a microfiche machine. A copying service is available on payment of a small fee per page.

Many trade directories are on the library shelves, filed alphabetically under the counties. There are London directories starting as early as 1677 and a collection of Dublin directories covering nine years from 1747.

Other subjects covered are schools and universities with an extensive collection of registers. Directories and registries of professions including law lists of solicitors and barristers from 1813, clergymen, doctors and surgeons, judges, architects, musicians and many more.

As you will appreciate, there is a wealth of information to be gained from a visit to the Society of Genealogists. By using the library, in one day you might possibly save yourself several separate visits to more distant research repositories or could at least form some idea of whether a visit would prove fruitful. The library, which is closed on Mondays, is open on other days for as many as 8 hours giving you the advantage of a good long day for research. In order to make the best use of the Society's library, make a list of all the names or subjects you wish to research and follow it closely. You may be tempted, but unless you have a spare day on which to indulge yourself, do not dip into books that attract your attention or you will be side-tracked and not look for all you are seeking, as I know to my cost. The Society's library is an Aladdin's Cave of genealogical and historical data.

The library is arranged on three floors. Researchers are requested not to take bags and briefcases into the reading rooms and a cloakroom with lockers is provided on the ground floor.

The ground floor is the Lower Library which holds miscellaneous card indexes, the I.G.I. and microfilm collection together with the microfilm and microfiche machines, catalogues for the films and the microfiche. There is also what is known as "The Great Card Index" which contains several million cards filed alphabetically by surname, giving any miscellaneous data that has been collected by the Society – a good place to start on your first visit.

On the first floor is the Middle Library where you will find an enquiry desk and all books on open shelves filed by county. There is also a separate section for the volumes of "Boyd's Citizens of London". There is a photocopying machine in the Middle Library. A small fee is charged for each photocopy. There is a card index catalogue of all the available material but if you require advice or something that is not on the shelves, the librarian at the desk will help. There are tables and chairs in this library for the use of members.

On the floor above is the Upper Library where there are the special document collections and family histories together with reference books relating to education, the armed forces, heraldry, overseas and "Boyd's Marriage Index". The document collection is on the left as you enter and consists of six sets of shelves reaching almost to the ceiling (ladder provided) full of boxes containing manuscript and typescript documents filed in envelopes under surnames in alphabetical order. Another interesting area for research for a first time visitor. There is a typed list of all the names on a table near the shelves. It is thought to contain about 11,000 names.

In the basement, in addition to the toilets there is a lecture room and a comfortable rest room where your own food may be consumed. Coffee and tea making facilities are provided for a small fee. There are also toilets on the other library floors and a book stall on the ground floor near the main entrance.

Guildhall Library

The Guildhall Library in London has a department devoted to genealogy, covering in detail the City of London, London Boroughs and the Greater London area together with information relating to other counties. There are no search fees, all that is required is a signature in the visitors' book at the enquiry desk in the manuscript room. There is usually an attendant on duty just inside the entrance to the library who will direct you to the manuscript room which is up a small flight of stairs to the left through the map room. To the right is the reference library. The manuscript room and library have a plentiful supply of desks and comfortable chairs for the use of readers.

The manuscript room, which has both microfilm and microfiche machines, has a collection on microfilm of the parish registers of the City of London, the London Boroughs, parts of Greater London and the County of Middlesex. They also have the microfiche of the I.G.I. covering the same areas. The microfiche for the British Isles are held in the library where there are several microfiche and microfilm machines available for use and it is not necessary to make an appointment. There are also copies of Census Records in the reference library. This is particularly helpful since you do not have to wait for the films to be brought to you, but can help yourself, and view them on the microfilm machines in the library room. Copying facilities are also available (again small change necessary).

There are extensive records relating to the City of London including City institutions such as the famous Goldsmiths and Silversmiths together with other less well known Guilds and Livery Companies with apprenticeship records, such as the Clock and Watchmakers and the Fishmongers. If you have an ancestor who was a tradesman or craftsman in the City of London these records are very helpful. There are Law Lists from 1787, records of the Royal College of Surgeons of England from 1518. There are records relating to the House of Commons, Old Bailey trials, naturalisation papers and Change of Name deeds.

Books on the shelves of the reference library cover a wide range. One of the largest collections of trade and street directories in the country is held by this library. Some on open shelves, some locked behind glass fronted shelves and others kept elsewhere on the premises. If you do not see the directories you require, ask at the desk where there are several archivists and librarians available to assist you. Tell them the number of the table where you are sitting and complete an application form and the books will be brought to you. There is a large card index of all the books and manuscripts available and if anything you wish to see is not readily available, ask at the desk. The archivists and librarians are very knowledgeable about the books on their shelves and very willing to help with problems. If they do not have the information on their own shelves, they will probably be able to direct you to another library or repository where you can find the information you are seeking.

In addition the reference library holds on microfilm a complete run of *The Times* newspaper.

City of London Corporation

The Records Office of the City of London Corporation is also in the Guildhall. This record office holds additional records relating specifically to the City of London.

Federation of Family History Societies

There are many Family History Societies throughout the country which come under the umbrella of the Federation. Most local societies concentrate on family history research within their own county and produce a regular journal relating to their work. If your research takes you outside the county in which you now live, write to the secretary of the society in the county you wish to research, giving the surname or place names in which you are interested. The local society may have someone amongst them who has been researching that name or can tell you about the place. If you join your own local society, they will exchange information through the Federation with other societies. The Federation also publish many useful booklets relating to different aspects of family history research. There is also a Guild of One Name Studies affiliated to the Federation, specialising in the study of one name only. If there is a society for your name, or any of the family names that you are researching, their research and publications may be of interest to you although they may not necessarily have any information relating to your particular family even if the name is the same.

Borthwick Institute of Historical Research, York

The Borthwick Institute in St. Anthony's Hall, York is a research institute of York University, and holds many original manuscripts which could help those in the north, who do not have the time and money to make protracted journeys to London. They specialise in the study of church history particularly in relation to administration and law in the northern province. The Institute is mainly for the use of research students, but it is open to the public. It is necessary to make an appointment in advance if you wish to carry out research on their archives. There is a room where readers can consume their own food and facilities for making tea and coffee supplied for a small charge. There is also a copying service available for some classes of documents.

The library known as the Gurney Library holds approximately 14,000 books on its shelves, relating to all aspects of historic research including local societies and most record offices. Copy parish registers, probate records and Bishops' transcripts are held as are original manuscripts and typescripts deposited by private families and individuals relating to Yorkshire and Nottinghamshire. Estate records, Charity papers, school records, and wills are also available. It is advisable to enquire whether they hold the documentation you are seeking before embarking on an appointment to carry out research. The Institute publish a helpful guide giving details of their genealogical sources which may be of assistance to family historians. The Institute specialise in document conservation and restoration and if you can take a tour of their work and conservation rooms I would urge you to do so. You will be privileged to see many famous early documents and manuscripts and the meticulous loving care and scientific research carried on by the "backroom boys" at the Institute.

The Newspaper Library

The Newspaper Library at Colindale is a branch of the British Library where you can research amongst nearly 600,000 volumes, and 220,000 microfilms housed on about 18 miles of shelving. Their stock is increased each year with up to date newspapers, but it is the past that will interest you more. It is easy to reach, being almost opposite the Colindale underground station which is on the Northern line. There is also a small car park.

Admission to the library is free. It is restricted to those over 21 years of age and it is necessary to obtain a reader's ticket by producing proof of your identity. The library suggest that you telephone before you visit them, in order to ascertain that they hold the information you require and what proof of your identity you will be asked to supply. There are over 100 seats for readers including more than 30 with microfilm machines. There is a catalogue of all the newspapers in a card index and in loose leaf folders together with indexes to *The Times* and the *New York Times*. The library offers copying facilities and will also supply copies by post if you can give them an exact reference of the piece you are seeking. There is a refreshment room with drinks and food vending machines where you can also eat your own food.

The newspaper collections dating from 1800 are daily and weekly papers and periodicals including London newspapers. Provincial, Welsh, Scottish and Irish newspapers are held dating from 1700 as well as foreign newspapers. There is also a collection of printed books relating to the newspaper industry, journalism and the history of the press.

India Office Library

Many of us have ancestors who were connected with India, either through work or through the armed forces. Young men set out for India to make their fortunes by working for the British East India Company or joined regiments of the army which were based in India. There they married, had families and often died. Some fell in love with the country and on discharge from the army remained there to work on the railway. All those lives were well documented and the records are today held in the India Office Library which is at 197 Blackfriars Road, London.

The library which is on the fourth floor consists of a catalogue room, and a readers' room. Admission, which is free, is by a reader's day pass which is obtained by signing the visitors' book on the ground floor. Bags and briefcases may not be taken into the library, but there is a cloakroom inside the entrance to the catalogue room and an attendant will give you a numbered disc in exchange for your bags and coat. An enquiry desk in the catalogue room is manned by very helpful librarians and archivists. There are a number of tables in the reading room and it is necessary to obtain a seat with a number so that you can give the number of the seat when you order a book or document which will be brought to you, normally very quickly. Reference numbers of documents and books can be obtained from the indexes in the catalogue room and entered on printed forms together with your seat number which are then handed to the desk. The use of pencils only rule is strictly enforced and if you should forget your "travel pack" this is one of the libraries where you can purchase pencils. All materials should be returned to the desk after use. The library offers copying facilities and a printed leaflet gives details of costs and procedures. There is a refreshment room on the 11th floor where there are drink vending machines and you may eat your own food.

The library publish a number of free guides giving details of the collections they hold and how to gain access to them. There is also a guide to the library which is in the catalogue room.

The extensive records which are of most interest to the family historian are the ecclesiastical and army records giving details of births, marriages and deaths, service records both civil and military, wills, probate and pension funds. They cover The East India Company from 1600 to 1858, the Board of Control from 1784 to 1858, The India Office from 1858 to 1947 and the Burma Office from 1937 to 1948. The records cover much written material, that which was sent to India from England and that sent to England from India. They cover not only India, but parts of Burma, Indonesia, Malaysia, St. Helena, China and Japan. An interesting item amongst the records of St. Helena is the death certificate of Napoleon Bonaparte. Unfortunately in 1858 many records were disposed of as "waste paper" and were sold to a dealer. Fortunately the dealer realised how important the "waste paper" was and spent the next fifty years selling the records back to the India Office so all was not lost.

Trade Museums and Libraries

There are very many museums and libraries devoted to one subject, tucked away in back streets, not necessarily in London but all over the country. If by tradition your family or ancestors specialised in a particular trade or interest, passing down their knowledge from father to son over the ages there is probably a museum for you somewhere, where you might find specific reference to your family name. You may even find photographs amongst their archives. Most of the Guilds and Livery Halls in the City of London have museums. If your ancestors were stonemasons, or train drivers, worked in the potteries, were butchers, glass blowers, doctors, carpenters, or opera singers, there are collections of records looked after by devoted archivists somewhere waiting for you. It is well worth making enquiries. Your local library should have a

copy of the "Museum Year Book" which gives all the
museums in the British Isles with addresses, telephone
numbers and hours of opening.

There is a Mining Museum in Stoke on Trent, a
Bagpipe Museum in Morpeth, a Museum for Chartered
Insurance in London and a Historical Exhibition of the
British Red Cross in Guildford in Surrey. Principal
museums in cities and large towns mount special exhibi-
tions from time to time. Watch out for announcements
and articles in the local or national press. The subjects are
varied, some local and some based on international
events, but many are of interest to the family historian. St.
Paul's Cathedral in London had an exhibition of Jewish
records in the crypt, showing many early photographs.
The Print Library in a small back street near St. Bride's in
London have a permanent collection related to all aspects
of the paper trade, including the manufacture and printing
of paper and books. I was directed to that particular
library by a librarian at the Guildhall Library when I was
researching someone connected with the paper trade. The
archivist was very helpful and eventually found a collection of house magazines for the company where the
person concerned had been an apprentice. In one of those
little booklets I found a detailed written history giving his
full name and date of birth, his father's name, their
address at the signing of the indentures together with a
history of his rise in the company's employment and
details of his marriage and his children. A really wonder-
ful find!

There is also an excellent series of books divided into
geographical areas, published by H.M.S.O., giving full
details of most museums.

13

BOOK ONE OF YOUR FAMILY HISTORY

One of the pleasures of tracing your family history is the fact that you can take a rest whenever you wish and return to it at any time. Some of those "bitten by the bug" spend most of their leisure time working at their family history, often using their weekends and annual holidays to visit archives, record offices and registries or the places where their forebears originated. For those living in England whose forebears originated elsewhere, a visit to Ireland, Wales, Scotland or even further can combine a very pleasant holiday with an opportunity to continue the research. The Society of Genealogists and the Federation of Family History Societies offer interesting and valuable evening classes, weekend and week long seminars and conferences. A few days spent in the company of dedicated family historians and genealogists gives renewed energy and determination to continue. And what a lot you can learn in those few days! If you have become a member of the Society of Genealogists you will receive information of all lectures, seminars and conferences. If not, write at the beginning of the year to ask them for their programme so that you can plan any trips you wish to make.

Once you have found addresses where your forebears lived and the locations of some of their burials, visit the places if you can, taking your camera or persuade a photographer friend to accompany you. Some of the houses and buildings mentioned in your documentation may have disappeared by now. In towns and cities whole streets of houses have been demolished to make way for modern redevelopment and country areas are now crisscrossed by motorways. You may be lucky, however and find the house where a great great grandparent was born. I found one such house in a small town in Scotland. The male members of the family had been stonemasons through the ages and there was a carving over the front door of the house showing stonemasons' tools with the date 1720. I could picture George Thompson carefully carving that stone, little knowing how delighted one of his ancestors would be to find it 260 years later. A photograph of the house and the carving now form part of my documentation. I was also able to purchase a booklet, in a small local museum, giving the history of the area. All these things give depth and perspective to a family history. Visiting houses, towns and villages brings you closer to the people you are researching and makes you aware of the pleasures and difficulties of their lives.

Visiting churchyards and cemeteries can also bring pleasure as well as sadness. Branches of families die out or move away leaving gravestones neglected. The weather and time are very destructive, but a tranquil picture of a churchyard, a memorial stone standing under a tree and a close-up of that stone will add greatly to the narrative of a family history.

If you should get a little bored ploughing your way through the indexes, take a rest and turn to other things. You have your records to keep up to date, a good task to undertake in the winter months when the nights are longer and travelling is not so easy. Your family chart should be revised and updated as you delve further into the past. You also have the task of bringing all the information together on paper.

Not all of you will wish to write a book, but page by page your manuscript will grow. Once you have sufficient information start to write your family history, which will eventually combine with your family tree, photographs, original and copy documents. Use a loose leaf ring binder adding separate pages as you write. You can also keep them in chronological order, inserting them in the correct place without difficulty.

Although you are writing the story for yourself in order to bring together the results of your researches, it will undoubtedly be read by others. Members of your family will wish to read it and you may care to deposit a copy with the Society of Genealogists to assist the generations to come. Make it as interesting as you can. If you have the necessary information, describe what people looked like, the colour of their hair and eyes, how tall they were, together with a reference to any outstanding features. You will find that members of your family will sometimes be surprised by descriptions of their distant kinsmen and recognise in those descriptions likenesses to today's descendants.

Start by making notes of one person on the first sheet of paper. Try using yourself as the first person. What do you know? Your name – put that at the top of the page. On this page which is a guide for yourself on which to base the final manuscript, add your reference numbers so that you can refer to your records. The final manuscript does not need to show the reference numbers since they will become a distraction to anyone reading the family history. On each line underneath, add another piece of information, date of birth, place of birth, parents' names, schools attended, examinations passed, degrees won, interests and unusual hobbies, residences occupied with the dates of the moves. If you are married, the date and place of your marriage, the name of your spouse, the names and dates of birth of any children, present address. In the case of yourself, all these things will be known to you from memory, but you should support them with as much documentation as possible. When you write up the pages relating to your parents, grandparents and great grand-parents, most of your information will come from the results of your researches, and will also include the date and place of death. The longer they lived, the more infor-

mation you should have. These notes will form the bare
branches on which the leaves will grow.

The following is a copy of the first notes made relating
to a member of my family whom I knew and who was able
personally to give me many details on which to base my
researches. It is therefore recent history:

Fanny Rayner (A1)
Born: 7 May 1896, Bilgoraj, Poland
Parents: Maurice Rayner (A3), Esther? (M36)
Schools: Hackney Primary, Green's Grammar School,
Stepney.
Residence: 306 Wick Road, Hackney
Occupation: hairdresser
Married: 18 October 1926 Hackney Registry Office
Alfred Gennings (S4) – Occupation: Engineer
Present: Rebecca Gosman and William Edward Gennings
(S7) (Groom's brother)
Female Child born 3 October 1928 Elizabeth Esther (S12)
Residences: 1926–1929 21 Greenwood Road, Hackney
   1930–1940 91 Farley Road, Stoke Newington
   1941–1949 9 Wellington Road, Leyton
   1950–1965 33 Naverino Road, Hackney
   1966–1979 18 Kirkstead Court, Hackney
Died: 21 November 1979

All the necessary facts are there, but how bleak and
uninteresting. The following page is the beginning of the
rounded out history of Fanny Rayner:

"Fanny Rayner, the daughter of Maurice and Esther was
born in Bilgoraj, Poland on 7 May 1896. The maiden name
of Esther is not known since no birth certificate is known
to exist for Fanny but an Affidavit sworn by her father in
January 1956 gives the details of her birth. Maurice and
Esther with Fanny emigrated to England in 1900.

The family lived at 306 Wick Road in a prosperous part
of the London Borough of Hackney over the hairdresser's
establishment opened by Maurice where he catered for

the local population, both men and women. The shop was well situated between a public house and a grocer's store, close to Victoria Park, in an area comprising both shopping and residential accommodation. Fanny attended the local primary school and gained a scholarship to Sir George Green's Grammar School in Stepney. She remained at the school until the age of 16 and then joined her father in his shop as an apprentice hairdresser. Fanny was 5ft 2in tall, had dark hair and brown eyes. At the age of 28 years on 18 October 1926, Fanny married Alfred Gennings an engineer, of 9 Etropol Road, Hackney. The witnesses to the marriage were Rebecca Gosman, a friend of Fanny, and William Edward Gennings, Alfred's younger brother. Fanny ceased her occupation as a hairdresser and took up residence with her husband Alfred in rented accommodation at 21 Greenwood Road, Hackney where they were living when her only child, a daughter, Elizabeth Esther was born at the Mother's Hospital in Hackney on 3 October 1928. Elizabeth Esther weighing only 4½ lb at birth was born prematurely and Fanny was unable to have any more children.

Fanny remained at home looking after her family while Alfred continued to work as an engineer. They moved house in 1930 to 91 Farley Road, Stoke Newington, once again in rented accommodation. Fanny became a voluntary school assistant in 1935 at Upton House School, Hackney and a School Governor in 1937. In 1939 she assisted with the evacuation of the children of Upton House School to Thetford in Norfolk, where she remained for a year acting as a liaison between the children, their parents and the local population. Later she returned to London to work in a munitions factory . . ." and so the story continues until her death in 1979.

The story is Fanny's with references to her father, mother, daughter and brother-in-law. Her parents Maurice and Esther each have their own page and story, as do her husband Alfred and her daughter Elizabeth Esther. Elizabeth Esther's children and grandchildren also make an appearance further on in the saga. Fanny's story is by no means complete. You will have noticed that there is a gap between her age at 16 and at 28. Other parts of her early life are only sketched in with the information at present known. There is a need for much more research. So it always will be with family history and genealogy – a never ending journey.

The documents supporting this part of the family history are the original Affidavit of her father, three school reports, a photograph of Fanny standing on the doorstep of her father's shop. Her original marriage certificate, letters written from Thetford in Norfolk, a photograph of a group of factory munition workers, and her death certificate.

You may notice that Fanny's date of birth of May 1896 does not agree with her age at her marriage. Perhaps her father was mistaken about her date of birth or the incorrect age was entered on her marriage certificate. This is just one example of the inconsistencies that you may find as you research your family history.

The following are brief extracts from manuscripts written by a family historian in 1850 which were given to me as part of the family documentation of a family for whom I prepared a family history. The style of writing is very different from that used today and very little detail is given, but the writer conveys to the reader his sensitivity and the tender feelings he still held for his deceased wife. The first and second refer to one of his relations and the third although apparently written from a distance, to his own wife.

"Angus Bantry son of Johnathan Bantry a yeoman of Eden End Northamptonshire and grandson of Samuel Bantry was sent to Highcroft school with the idea of being a farmer, but not liking it, and farming being bad, he came to Manchester as a boy of fifteen with ten shillings in his pocket and obtained a post in a bank and became rich."

The second by Angus himself refers to a letter he received from a clergyman.

"This letter from Rev Mr. Tree the clergyman then residing at Eden End was written about the 12th January 1808 and the half guinea enclosed to me was all my capital for starting life. Before my good father left me in Manchester he gave me a five pound note because at that time I had no salary from the Banking House and to the best of my recollection I never received further assistance from him or any one else."

The third written by Daniel Bantry.

"Alice the beloved wife of Daniel Bantry was the eldest daughter of Thomas and Nancy Harding and was born at their house in Manchester on March 22nd 1793. She was married on April 9th 1817 and soon afterwards attended at Chapel and was with her husband baptised June 30th 1821. Eighteen years before her decease her growing afflictions prevented her from regular attendance on the means of grace and for the last ten years of her life she was almost entirely confined to her habitation. She suffered most patiently from what was supposed a heart disease and died on November 3rd 1850. She was buried in Oldham cemetery in a family grave which is indicated by a neat marble monument."

These pages including the one from my own Family History give an idea of how to begin writing your own Family History. Develop your own style and add to your manuscripts as your research progresses.

Having conveyed to you the enjoyment and pleasure that can be derived from the pursuit of family history, I wish you success and leave you to draw up your own tree. There are many elements of family history research that

I have not dealt with and some that have been mentioned only in passing. Inevitably you will have many questions you would like to ask. There is more detailed information relating to the I.G.I., museums and the P.R.O. and I am conscious of the fact that I have not dealt with the meaning of names, nor how to find your ancestors if they were originally immigrants or if they emigrated. I am sure, however, that I have given you more than enough to whet your appetite and keep you occupied and your own researches will lead you to many answers.

One more thing before we part company. I realise I have made the point many times, but record offices, museums and repositories do change their hours of opening and sometimes have to close for stocktaking, conservation or redecoration. Please do telephone in advance to check times and availability of records so as to avoid a wasted journey.

APPENDIX

Useful names and addresses, telephone numbers and hours of opening (all liable to change with the passage of time).

Be aware of local Bank Holiday variations.

Registries

England and Wales
The General Register Office
St. Catherine's House
10 Kingsway
London WC2B 6JP
Tel: 0171 242 0262
Open: Monday–Friday 8.30am–4.30p.m.
Closed: Saturday, Sunday, Bank Holidays.
No entrance fee.
Certificates: personal application £6
            postal application £11.50 (no search)
                           £15.50 (with search)

Postal applications to:
OPCS GRO
Smedley Hydro
Southport
Merseyside PR8 2HH

Scotland
General Registry Office
New Register House
Edinburgh EH1 3YT
Tel: 0131 334 0380
Open: Monday–Thursday 9.00am–4.30pm
        Friday 9.00am–4.00pm
Closed: Saturday, Sunday, Bank Holidays.
Search fees: daily £12 or £16, weekly £60
            monthly £185, yearly £1,250
Appointment necessary.
Certificates: personal application £10
            postal application £12

Glasgow Office:
General Registrar
Marriage Suites
22 Park Circus
Glasgow G3
Tel: 0141 249 4500

Eire
General Registry Office
James Joyce House
8–11 Lombard Street
Dublin 2
Eire
Tel: 00 353 1 671 1000
Open: Monday–Friday 9.30am–4.30pm
Closed: Lunch daily 12.30pm–2.15pm, Saturday, Sunday,
        Bank Holidays.
Search fees: daily IR£12
                one search for five years IR£1.50
Photocopies: IR£1.50
Certificates: IR£5.50

Northern Ireland
Oxford House
49/55 Chichester Street
Belfast BT1 4HI
Northern Ireland
Tel: 01232 235211
Open: Monday–Friday 9.00am–4.30pm
Closed: Lunch daily 1pm–2.15pm, Sunday, Bank Holidays
No entrance fee charged

Isle of Man
General Registry
Finch Road
Douglas
Isle of Man
Tel: 01624 673358
Open: Monday–Saturday 9.00am–4.30pm
Closed: Lunch daily 1pm–2.15pm, Sunday, Bank Holidays

The Channel Islands
The Librarian
The Société Jersiaise
9 Pier Road, St. Helier
Jersey, Channel Islands
Tel: 01534 75940
Open: Monday–Saturday 10.00am–4.00pm winter
                        10.00am–5.00pm summer
        Sunday 1.00pm–4.00pm

Registrar General
States Building
Royal Square
St. Helier
Jersey, Channel Islands
Postal enquiries recommended.

Registrar General
Royal Court House
St. Peter Port
Guernsey, Channel Islands
Postal enquiries ONLY.

Principal Probate Registry
Somerset House
Strand
London WC2R 1LP
Tel: 0171 936 6000
Open: Monday–Friday 10.00am–4.30pm
Closed: Saturday, Sunday, Bank Holidays
Copying facilities.
No entrance fee.

Other useful addresses

Public Record Office
Chancery Lane
London WC2A 1LR
Tel: 0181 876 3444
Open: Monday–Friday
     9.30am–5.00pm
Closed: Saturday, Sunday,
    Bank Holidays, first
    two weeks in October
Reader's Ticket required –
  no charge.
Copying service.

Public Record Office
Ruskin Avenue
Kew
Richmond
Surrey TW9 4DU
Tel: 0181 876 3444
Open: Monday–Saturday
     9.30am–5.00pm
Closed: Sunday, Bank
    Holidays
Reader's ticket required –
  no charge.
Copying service.

Public Record Office of Northern Ireland
66 Balmoral Avenue
Belfast
Northern Ireland

National Archives (Ireland)
Bishops Street
Dublin 8
Eire
Tel: 00 353 1 478 3711
Open: Monday-Friday 10.00am–5.00pm
Closed: Saturday, Sunday, Bank Holidays

Registry of Deeds (Ireland)
Henrietta Street
Dublin 1
Eire

British Museum Library
Great Russell Street
London WC1B 3DG
Tel: 0171 636 1544
Recorded information: 0171 580 1788
Reader's Ticket required – no charge.

National Museum of Wales
Cathays Park
Cardiff CF1 3NP

National Library, Dublin
Kildare Street
Dublin 2
Eire
Open: Monday 10.00am–9.00pm
    Tuesday/Wednesday 2.00pm–9.00pm
    Thursday/Friday 10.00am–5.00pm
    Saturday 10.00am–1.00pm
Tel: 00 353 1 661 8811

Mid Glamorgan County
  Library
Coed Parc, Park Street
Bridgend CF31 4BA

National Library of Wales
Aberystwyth
Dyfed SY23 3BU
Tel: 01970 623816

National Library of Scotland
George IV Bridge
Edinburgh EH1 1EW
Tel: 0131 226 4531

Genealogical Office (Ireland)
Kildare Street
Dublin 2
Eire
Personal Consultancy Service
Monday–Friday 10.00am–12.30pm
                    2.00pm–4.00pm
Fees: IR£20.00 per hour
Tel: 00 353 1 661 8811 ex. 402

Borthwick Institute of Historical Research
St. Anthony's Hall
York YO1 2PW
Tel: 01904 642315
Open: Monday–Friday 9.30am–5.00pm
Closed: Lunch daily 1.00pm–2.00pm, Saturday, Sunday,
        Bank Holidays, two weeks in August
Copying facilities.
Appointment necessary.

Guildhall Library
Aldermanbury
London EC2P 2EJ
Tel: 0171 606 3030
Open: Monday–Saturday
          9.30am–5.00pm
Closed: Sunday,
        Bank Holidays
Copying service.
No entrance fee.

British Red Cross
Archives and Historical
   Exhibition
Guildford
Surrey
Tel: 01483 898595
Appointment necessary

India Office Library
197 Blackfriars Road
London SE1 8NG
Tel: 0171 928 9531
Open: Monday–Friday
          9.30am–5.45pm
      Saturday
          9.30am–1.45pm
Closed: Sunday, Bank Holidays
Copying facilities.
Day pass – no charge.

Newspaper Library
Colindale Avenue
London NW9 5HE
Open: Monday–Saturday
          10.00am–4.45pm
Closed: Sunday, Bank Hols,
        1 week in October
Copying facilities.
Reader's Ticket required.
No charges.

St. Brides Printing Library
Bride Lane
London EC4Y 8EE
Tel: 0171 353 4660
Open: Monday–Friday 9.30am–5.30pm
Closed: Saturday, Sunday, Bank Holidays
Copying facilities.
No charge.

Manx Museum
Kingswood Grove
Douglas
Isle of Man IM1
Tel: 01624 675522
Open: Monday-Saturday
      10.00am–5.00pm
Closed: Sunday and Bank Holidays

Morpeth Chantry Bagpipe Museum
Bridge Street
Morpeth
Northumberland NE61 1PJ
Tel: 01670 519466

Museum of Mining
Chatterley Whitfield Colliery
Tunstall
Stoke on Trent
Tel: 01782 813337
Open: Daily 10.00am–4.00pm
Entrance fee.

Museum of Chartered Insurance Institute
20 Aldermanbury
London EC2V 7HY
Tel: 0171 606 3835

Baptist Union
129 The Broadway
Didcot
Oxon OX11 8XB
Tel: 01235 512007

Huguenot Library
University Library
Gower Street
London WC1
Tel: 0171 380 7094

Catholic Central Library
17 Francis Street
London SW1P 1DN

Catholic Family History Society
Secretary: Mrs Barbara Murray
2 Winscombe Crescent
Ealing
London W5 1AZ
Annual subscription: £6

Jewish Museum
Woburn House
Tavistock Square
London WC1H 0EP
Tel: 0171 388 4525

Mormon Branch Library
LDS Chapel
401 Holywood Road
Belfast BT4 2GU
Northern Ireland
Tel: 01232 768250

Presbyterian Historical Society and
 United Reform Church History Society
86 Tavistock Place
London WC1H 9RT
Tel: 0171 837 7661

Society of Friends Library
Friends House
Euston Road
London NW1
Tel: 0171 387 3601

Society of Genealogists
14 Charterhouse Buildings
Goswell Road
London EC1M 7AB
Tel: 0171 251 8799
Open: Tuesday, Friday, Saturday 10.00am–6.00pm
       Wednesday, Thursday 10.00am–8.00pm
Closed: Monday, Bank Holidays (and Friday previous),
        one week in February
Search fees: £3.00 per hour
             £7.50 for 4 hours
             £10.00 per day
No fees to members.

Professional Researchers

Association of Genealogists
 and Record Agents (AGRA)
The Secretary
29 Badgers Close
Horsham
West Sussex RH12 5RU

Association of Professional
 Genealogists (APG)
4321 M Street N.W.
Suite 236
Washington DC 20007
USA

Paul Gorry
Gorry Research
12 Burrow Road
Sutton
Dublin 13
Eire
Tel: 00 353 1 393942

Mrs Sandra Speedie
57 Dunellan Road
Milngavie
Glasgow G62 7RE
Tel: 0141 956 7050

Stephen T J Wright
4 Rose Glen
Chelmsford CM2 9EN
Tel: 01245 259965

REGNAL TABLE

Monarch	Years of Reign			
William I	25 December	1066–	25 September	1087
William II	26 September	1087–	4 August	1100
Henry I	5 August	1100–	25 December	1135
Stephen	26 December	1135–	18 December	1154
Henry II	19 December	1154–	2 September	1189
Richard I	3 September	1188–	26 May	1199
John	27 May	1199–	27 October	1216*
Henry III	28 October	1216–	19 November	1272
Edward I	20 November	1272–	7 July	1307
Edward II	8 July	1307–	24 January	1327
Edward III	25 January	1327–	21 June	1377
Richard II	22 June	1377–	29 September	1399
Henry IV	30 September	1399–	20 March	1413
Henry V	21 March	1413–	31 August	1422
Henry VI	1 September	1422–	3 March	1461
Edward IV	4 March	1461–	8 April	1483
Edward V	9 April	1483–	25 June	1483
Richard III	26 June	1483–	21 August	1485
Henry VII	22 August	1485–	21 April	1509
Henry VIII	22 April	1509–	27 January	1547
Edward VI	28 January	1547–	26 June	1553
Lady Jane Grey	27 June	1553–	nine days	
Mary I	6 July	1553–	24 July	1554
Philip & Mary	25 July	1554–	16 November	1558
Elizabeth I	17 November	1558–	23 March	1603
James I	24 March	1603–	26 March	1625
Charles I	27 March	1625–	18 May	1649
Commonwealth Interregnum 1649–1660				
Charles II	30 January	1649–	5 February	1685
James II	6 February	1685–	11 December	1688
Interregnum 12 December 1688–12 February 1689				
William III & Mary	13 February	1689–	27 December	1694
William III	28 December	1694–	7 March	1702
Anne	8 March	1702–	31 July	1714
George I	1 August	1714–	10 June	1727
George II	11 June	1727–	24 October	1760
George III	25 October	1760–	28 January	1820
George IV	29 January	1820–	25 June	1830
William IV	26 June	1830–	19 June	1837
Victoria	20 June	1837	use of regnal years discontinued	

*King John regnal years were calculated from Ascension day each year.

INDEX